CONTENTS

KU-126-119

IBIZA & FORMENTERA

Only the unacquainted could dismiss Ibiza as little more than a ravers' paradise and those who know the island well know it to be one of Spain's most cosmopolitan and attractive corners – affluent, self-confident, and with a fascinating heritage and a vibrant, home-grown music scene of global reach and importance.

Las Salinas Beach

Ibiza architecture

A pivotal part of the Carthaginian empire between 600 and 50 BC, Ibiza was closely linked with the fertility goddess Tanit and the god of dance Bes (from whom the name Ibiza is derived). Its status, however, declined under Roman occupation, and the island spent the next two thousand years as a backwater. Then, in the early 1960s, political opponents of Franco settled here and waves of beatniks discovered the island. **Ibiza**'s decidedly bohemian character is rooted in this era, and remains particularly evident in the north of the island, where you'll find ethnic bazaars and hippy markets, as well as a large population of alternative types.

The island's natural beauty is captivating. Large swathes of the coastline survive in pristine condition, with sweeping sandy bays and exquisite coves tucked beneath soaring cliffs. Ibiza's hilly, thickly wooded interior is peppered with isolated whitewashed villages and terraced fields of almonds, figs and olives. To really experience the scenic beauty and tranquility of the island's countryside, stay at an *agroturimo* (rural hotel) for a while; many excellent new places have opened in the last few years.

What's new

Recent years have seen an increase in outdoor, daytime parties challenging the post-midnight clubs of old, with the rising popularity of **pool parties** and **beach clubs** sucking up ever more tourist euros. Musically, clubs and venues are broadening their horizons, with grime, rap and UKG getting more playtime, as well as funk and disco, instead of just the usual house and techno. Behind the scenes, dramatic **rental increases** on both islands mean seasonal workers can't afford a home, potentially leaving many venues without a full complement of staff.

When to visit

Ibiza and Formentera are very warm between June and late September, when cloudless skies are virtually guaranteed. The heat can get intense in July and August, when highs in the 30s are common, but even at this time of year cooling sea breezes usually intervene to prevent things getting too uncomfortable. Winter in the Pitiuses (southern Balearics) is also glorious, with very little rainfall and temperatures normally high enough to enjoy sitting outside in cafés, even in January. As far as crowds go, there's a very clearly defined tourist season on both islands that begins slowly around Easter, peaks in August when the islands get really packed, and slowly winds down from late September and throughout October. Winter is a wonderfully peaceful time for a visit, with late January and early February a particularly beautiful time to come. Nightlife might be thin on the ground, but the skies are still blue and the almond trees and winter wild flowers are in full bloom.

Experimental Beach

The charismatic capital, **Ibiza Town**, harbours most of the island's architectural treats, including a spectacular walled enclave, Dalt Vila, and a port area stuffed with hip bars, stylish restaurants and fashionable boutiques. Laying claim to be the world's clubbing capital, Ibiza is an incredibly hedonistic place, where the nights are celebrated with unique spirit in landmark clubs scattered across the southern half of the island.

Serene, easy-going **Formentera**, the other main island of the Pitiuses (southern Balearics), is just a short ferry ride south of Ibiza yet offers a complete contrast. Boasting a relaxed, unhurried atmosphere and miles of ravishing sandy beaches lapped by translucent water, it has little or no nightlife and few historical sights apart from some sombre fortress churches and minor archeological ruins. It's the simplicity of life here, a back-to-nature appeal, which is Formentera's real allure.

Language

Catalan, not Castilian Spanish, is the official language of the islands, and we have therefore used Catalan names throughout the guide.

Where to...

Shop

There are some great boutiques around La Marina, Sa Penya and Vara de Rey, where you'll find interesting vintage, designer and curio shops among the slew of t-shirt and trinket vendors. Elsewhere around the islands, hippy markets selling quality, handmade goods are popular, while a couple of large, eccentric shopping emporiums have popped up on the road to Santa Gertrudis. Shopping in Formentera is limited and the shops around the main square in Sant Francesc are your best bet.

OUR FAVOURITES: Sluiz, see page 65. Vino & Co., see page 93. Holala!, see page 38.

Eat

Ibiza Town is the main draw, with plenty of hip cafés and chic restaurants clustered around La Marina, Sa Penya and Dalt Vila, while nearby Talamanca is great for seafood tapas. Santa Eulària has its own 'restaurant street', Carrer Sant Vicent, and a lively port with some decent dining options in summer. San An can hardly be described as a foodie haven but you can eat well along the harbourfront and just outside town. Santa Gertrudis is home to a bewildering number of restaurants given its diminutive size, while the variety of restaurants along the Sant Llorenç–Sant Joan road make it another dining hotspot. Formentera is Ibiza in miniature, with the same range and variety of eating options, albeit on a smaller scale.

OUR FAVOURITES: Bon Sol, see page 93. La Paloma, see page 66. Beso Beach, see page 109.

Drink

In Spain, drinking and eating are rarely separated and most bars offer food of some kind, even if just tapas or snacks. For exclusive drinking and bar hopping, head to Sa Penya and La Marina in Ibiza Town. Sant Antoni 's stylish bars lining the promenade connect the Sunset Strip with Caló des Moro, which are particularly appealing at sunset. Santa Eulària has more of a family vibe, with a focus on restaurants rather than bars, while other towns in the north, such as Sant Joan or Sant Miquel, are positively dead past midnight.

OUR FAVOURITES: Paradise Lost, see page 41. Teatro Pereyra, see page 42. Experimental Beach, see page 94.

Go out

For a gentle introduction, start with *Pacha* in Marina Botafoc, while nearby *Heart* offers the option to combine dancing with dinner and a show. San An's clubs tend to be cheap and cheerful and draw a younger crowd. Platja d'en Bossa is home to *Ushuaïa* and *Hï*, while clubbing titans *Privilege* and *Amnesia* are further afield outside Sant Rafel. For a more hard-core, less hyped experience, head to *DC10* on the Ses Salines road, or *Underground* in Sant Rafel. The only real nightlife in northeast Ibiza is at *Las Dalias*, while sleepy Formentera's two clubs are both in Es Pujols.

OUR FAVOURITES: Pikes, see page 81. Hï, see page 97. Underground, see page 81.

Ibiza and Formentera events calendar

Throughout the year, Ibiza and Formentera are host to some wonderfully diverse events, from cutting-edge music festivals to natural wonders. It's not possible to list them all, but below are some of our favourites, some of which may well be worth planning a trip around. The Essentials section (see page 130) details traditional and religious local festivals.

ALMOND BLOSSOM
Late January to early February
Crisp winter days are ideal for walking, especially from late January when the almond trees are in bloom and the islands take on a pinky-white hue, particularly around Santa Agnès in Ibiza (see page 64). Better yet, walk at night to see them by the light of the moon.

CARNIVAL
February
Towns and villages on both islands live it up during the week before Lent with marches, fancy-dress parades and classical music concerts, with the best displays on show in Ibiza Town (see page 26).

CALÇOTADA
February to April
The annual calçot harvest takes place in late winter and is celebrated every other Sunday at Bar Can Berri (see page 93) with a large barbecue, live music and dancing.

FLOWER POWER
Early March
Ibiza's psychedelic hippy heritage is commemorated with flowers, rainbows, outrageous costumes and an enormous party in the village of Sant Josep (see page 82).

ATZARÓ SPRING PARTY
End March
The lush gardens of Atzaró (see page 8) are the perfect setting for this much anticipated annual celebration of the arrival of spring, with live music, food and market stalls, holistic workshops and plenty of fun for kids.

MEDIEVAL FAIR
Second week in May
Dalt Vila turns back the clock in celebration of its Phoenician, Roman, Arabic and Christian past, and for a week the old town is home to knights, princesses, wizards and dragons, with colourful market stalls, medieval music, spit roasts, tournaments, parades and magic shows (see page 29).

INTERNATIONAL MUSIC SUMMIT
End of May

Three-day event featuring seminars and debates from leading influencers in the electronic music community, culminating in breath-taking shows in Dalt Vila (see page 29).

FORMENTERA JAZZ FESTIVAL
First weekend in June

Four days of workshops, concerts, DJ and jam sessions from local, national and international artists, with most activities taking place between the Jardí de ses Eres and the Plaça de sa Constitució in Sant Ferran (see page 104).

IBIZA GAY PRIDE
Mid-June

Fabulous four-day event with exhibitions, concerts and special club nights culminating in the exuberant last-day Grand Parade around the streets of Ibiza Town (see page 26).

PERSEID METEOR SHOWER
Mid-July to mid-August

Ibiza and Formentera's clear skies are ideal for star gazing, no more so than during the annual Perseid shower which peaks around the 11–13th August. Grab a blanket, find a hilltop and enjoy the show.

IBIZA LIGHT FESTIVAL
Mid-October

For two nights, the most emblematic parts of Ibiza's old port are transformed by light, video and audio artists and designers as part of a cultural project celebrating light, art and technology.

HALLOWEEN
31st October

Forget the club opening and closing parties, Halloween is officially *the* biggest party night of the year in Ibiza, with both venues and punters relishing the ghoulish theme to the max.

SANT MATEU WINE FESTIVAL
First weekend in December

A tremendously sociable event, with crowds sampling the local vintages and feasting on barbecued *sobrassada* and *butifarra* sausages, cooked over tin baths (see page 63).

CAP D'ANY
New Year's Eve

Traditionally celebrated in Spain by eating twelve grapes, one on each strike of the clock at midnight. Ibiza celebrates with big parties in all the clubs and a street party on Vara de Rey (see page 34).

Ibiza and Formentera at a glance

Ibiza

The northwest p.56.

The least populated part of the island, with a mix of pine-forested hills and rust-red terraced fields interspersed by diminutive villages. The undeveloped coastline of isolated coves, rugged cliffs and lonely stone watchtowers is a hiker's delight.

Santa Agnès

Sant Mateu d'Albarca

sa Galera

Conillera

Cala Gració

Sant Antoni Bay

Sant Antoni

CALA D'HORT NATURE PARK

s'Illa des Bosc

Port d'es Torrent

S'Estanyol

Sant Rafel

MEDITERRANEAN SEA

Cala Tarida

Sant Agustí

Cala Molí

Sant Josep

Cala Vedella

Cala Carbó

CALA D'HORT NATURE PARK

Cala d'Hort

Es Cubells

Sant Jordi

Sant Francesc

Es Vedra

SES SALINES NATURE PARK

Sant Antoni and around p.68.

Offering enough bars in its West End zone to drown the devil himself, popular clubs Eden and Es Paradis and the stylish lounge bars of the Sunset Strip, unpretentious Sant Antoni draws young clubbers in droves.

The south p.82.

Endowed with over a dozen bite-shaped calas (coves), the shimmering Salines salt flats and the remarkable soaring offshore islet of Es Vedrà, southern Ibiza's coastline is extraordinarily beguiling.

N

MEDITERRANEAN SEA

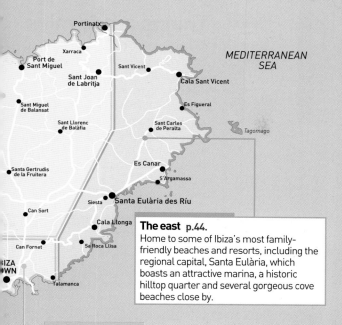

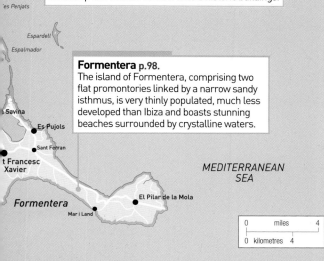

The east p.44.
Home to some of Ibiza's most family-friendly beaches and resorts, including the regional capital, Santa Eulària, which boasts an attractive marina, a historic hilltop quarter and several gorgeous cove beaches close by.

Ibiza Town and around p.26.
The island's vibrant, sassy capital is one of the most scenic ports in the Mediterranean. The colossal medieval walls of its old barrio, Dalt Vila (a UNESCO World Heritage Site), provide a startlingly evocative backdrop and contain most of Ibiza's historic buildings.

Formentera p.98.
The island of Formentera, comprising two flat promontories linked by a narrow sandy isthmus, is very thinly populated, much less developed than Ibiza and boasts stunning beaches surrounded by crystalline waters.

15

Things not to miss

It's not possible to see everything that Ibiza and Formentera has to offer in one trip – and we don't suggest you try. What follows is a selective taste of the islands' highlights, from secluded beaches to clubs and nightlife. All highlights are colour-coded by chapter and have a page reference to take you straight into the Guide, where you can find out more.

> Es Vedrà
See page 87
Looming above the southern coastline, this enigmatic 378m-high island looks magnificent from any angle.

< Sunset at Hostal La Torre
See page 117
Ibiza's thrills and spills do not come cheap, but, happily, the best spectacle of all is free.

∨ Clubbing
See page 43
House music's spiritual home, Ibiza serves up a selection of the globe's leading DJs virtually every night of the week in the summer months.

<**Pikes**
See page 81
Quirky, avant-garde boutique hotel
that's host to some of the best
party nights on the island.

∨ **Platja Illetes**
See page 105
The finest beach in the
Balearics, this sublime slender
finger of white sand lapped by
shallow pellucid waters lies at
Formentera's northern-most tip.

< **Cala Llentrisca**
See page 89
A short walk over a rocky headline keeps the masses away from this picture-perfect, secluded beach.

∨ **Hiking, Santa Agnès**
See page 62
One of Ibiza's most scenic sections of coastline, this path runs past steep cliffs and through terraced fields reclaimed by pine forests.

THINGS NOT TO MISS

∧ Las Dalias
See page 55
Famous hippy venue in Sant Carles hosting psych-trance and world music nights, plus a boho night market.

< Calle de la Virgen
See page 28
The heart of Ibiza's gay village, a historic portside street full of vibrant businesses and bars.

∧ Cycling in Formentera
See page 125
Flat and with a good network of signposted cycle routes, Formentera is great by bike.

∨ Kayak to Atlantis
See page 88
The perfect way to see Es Vedrà and visit the near-mythical cove of Atlantis is by kayak.

∧ **Dalt Vila**
See page 29
A focal point for the whole island, the capital's dramatic floodlit bastions and walls are visible for miles around.

< **Buillet de Peix at El Bigotes**
See page 53
Sample Ibiza's signature dish (fish stew and rice) at one of the east coast's most idyllic spots.

< **Portitxol**
See page 61
A startling horse-shoe shaped cove on Ibiza's most remote coastline.

∨ **Boat trip to Formentera**
See page 37
Only 28km separate Ibiza and Formentera and it's easy to charter a yacht, catamaran, speed boat or rib.

THINGS NOT TO MISS

Hidden Ibiza

Despite record numbers of visitors each year, it's still possible to escape the crowds, even in July and August. Though to get to some of the finest and most isolated spots, you may need to negotiate rough dirt roads and hike challenging rural paths.

Day one

Sa Talaia. See page 83. Start the day with an early morning hike up to Ibiza's highest point, Sa Talaia, for breath-taking views across the south of the island.

Es Cubells. See page 89. Driving to this pretty hamlet, home to a couple of decent café-restaurants and an impressive whitewashed church, is a pleasure in itself.

Cala Llentrisca. See page 89. The dramatic approach road from Es Cubells to Cala Llentrisca offers tempting glimpses of the turquoise waters and tranquillity to be found at this beautiful, secret beach.

🍴 **Lunch.** See page 94. Enjoy a long lunch of fresh fish or paella with terrific views at *Es Boldado*, just a short walk from Cala d'Hort.

Es Boldado

Atlantis. See page 88. A challenging walk is rewarded by translucent waters and other-worldly rock carvings and formations at this magical cove.

Sunset at Es Vedrà. See page 87. Feel the magnetic vibrations, or simply gawp in awe at this spectacular monolith silhouetted by technicolour sky, one of Ibiza's most iconic sights.

Atlantis

🍴 **Dinner.** See page 93. Dine under the stars and orange trees at the charming, laid-back and low-key restaurant *Bar Can Berri*, located in Sant Agustí, possibly one of Ibiza's prettiest villages.

Bar Can Berri

Day two

Cala Gració. See page 74. Start day two with an early morning swim in the beautifully calm and clear waters at pretty Cala Gració, or at its equally lovely sister, Cala Gracioneta. Both are blessed with soft, pale sand and sheltered waters and only really get busy later in the day in high season.

Las Puertas del Cielo. See page 66. A perfect example of the 'other' side of Ibiza; the beauty and isolation here are a world away from brash Platja d'en Bossa or Sant Antoni. And it's a great place for coffee and a snack.

Santa Agnès hike. See page 62. Remote coastal scenery, soaring cliffs plunging into turquoise waters, rich red earth and the scent of forest pines, plus the opportunity for a refreshing swim.

🍴 **Lunch.** See page 65. *Can Cires*, in charming, remote Sant Mateu, is known as the walkers' restaurant for good reason; the hearty Ibizan-Alsace fusion cuisine is ideal for big appetites.

Cala d'Albarca. See page 63. Getting to one of Ibiza's most remote and scenic spots requires some effort but the beauty and tranquillity of the surrounding landscape is well worth it.

Utopía Chiringuito. See page 67. People come and spend the whole day at this pretty cove, a short walk from Port de Sant Miguel, but it's great just for pre-dinner gin cocktails, or perhaps a jug of Cava sangría, too.

🍴 **Dinner.** See page 53. Deliberately difficult to find (but entirely possible via Google), the lovely converted farmhouse at *Can Suldat*, a short drive from Santa Eulària or Es Canar, is the ultimate hidden Ibiza dining experience.

Cala Gracioneta

Cala d'Albarca

Utopía Chiringuito

Kids' Ibiza & Formentera

Ibizans and Formenterans are extremely accommodating towards children, who are welcome in virtually all restaurants. With dozens of fine beaches and warm seas most of the year, plus a wide range of land- and water-based activities, children will be easily pleased.

Day one

Aguamar Water Park. See page 91. Water chutes and slides in all shapes and sizes, plus a large swimming pool, make for lots of splashy fun in Platja d'en Bossa.

Dramatised tour of Dalt Vila. See page 32. A trip back in time to the age of the Ibizan corsairs brings the history of the old town to life.

Aguamar Water Park

Day two

Aquarium Cap Blanc. See page 74. A smuggler's cave and lots of wriggly sea creatures will keep little human creatures amused, plus it's a lovely coastal walk to get here.

Glass-bottom boat tour from Sant Antoni. See page 68. A typical 3hr-trip takes in the beaches and coves all the way along the west coast to Es Vedrà, and includes drinks and snacks.

Glass-bottom boat

Day three

Tourist train to Portinatx. See page 123. All aboard this mock steam locomotive, a fantastic way to see the highlights and landscape of northern Ibiza.

Cova Can de Marçà. See page 61. The biggest cave system in Ibiza, and one of the stops on the Portinatx tourist train route. The guided tour culminates in an impressive light display, with a Tangerine Dream soundtrack.

Portinatx Express

Day four

Punta Arabí hippy market. See page 47. Kids will enjoy riffling for trinkets and souvenirs at the large weekly market just outside Es Canar on the east coast.

Cala Llonga. See page 44. Large, family-friendly beach offering plenty of water sports, plus a children's play area and small amusement park.

Day five

Horseriding. See page 127. Ibiza Horse Valley offers guided routes that take in the mountains and beaches of the north, and encourages riders to meet the horses and choose the one they feel comfortable with.

Lamuella. See page 67. Fabulous Asian-fusion restaurant near Sant Llorenç that goes out of its way to keep little ones entertained with a play area and creative workshops so grown-ups can relax.

Day six

Boat to Formentera. See page 27. With regular ferries leaving from Ibiza Town, Sant Antoni and Santa Eulària, it's easy to take a day-trip, or longer, to Ibiza's little sister island.

Rutas verdes. See page 122. Formentera's excellent network of cycling and hiking routes include shorter, gentler 30min options that take in the wildlife, lighthouses, pirate towers and windmills that children love.

Day seven

Go ape at Acrobosc. See page 47. Zip through the trees at this adventure park and assault course in S'Argamassa, near Es Canar.

Go-karting, Santa Eulària. See page 128. 300m track with bikes, carts and quads for all ages.

Punta Arabí hippy market

Horseriding on Ibiza

Cycling Formentera

PLACES

Statue in Ibiza Old Town

Ibiza Town and around

Set around a dazzling natural harbour, Ibiza Town (Eivissa) is one of the Mediterranean's most charismatic pocket-sized capitals, full of hip boutiques and chic bars and restaurants. Standing proud above the port is historic Dalt Vila, a rocky escarpment topped by a walled enclave. The fortress-like Catalan cathedral and craggy Moorish castle that bestride the summit are Ibiza's most famous landmarks, visible across much of the south of the island. Below Dalt Vila, Ibiza Town's harbour is the island's busiest, its azure waters ruffled by a succession of yachts, container ships and ferries. To the west is the boulevard-like Vara de Rey, while, occupying the north side of the bay, Marina Botafoc is an upmarket pleasure strip. Around Ibiza Town, you'll find a couple of decent beaches within easy reach.

La Marina

MAP P.28, POCKET MAP B7

La Marina, Ibiza Town's atmospheric harbourside district, often just referred to as *el puerto* ("the port"), is the heart of the Ibizan capital. A crooked warren of narrow streets, it's sandwiched between the harbour waters to the north and the walls of Dalt Vila in the south. Its alleys and tiny plazas are crammed with fashionable stores, restaurants and bars, and the almost souk-like streets fizz with life until the early hours during high season. By the middle of

La Marina

Arrival and information

A new **bus station**, just off the Can Misses roundabout, has been under construction for years, with no clear end in sight. Until it opens, all routes depart Ibiza Town from the bus stops along Av. d'Isidor Machabich and arrive on Av. d'Espanya. Buses run to/from the airport all year round (#10, every 20–30mins). Routes and times to all other destinations are included in the relevant entries in the text; you can also consult and download the latest timetables from ⓦ ibizabus.com. **Boats** (all May–Oct only) dock on the south side of the harbour for a number of destinations including Talamanca, Platja d'en Bossa and Santa Eulària. All boats to Formentera leave from a terminal on Av. Santa Eulària, on the west side of the harbour. There's a large car park off Av. Santa Eulària, but note charges rise up to €3.60 per hour after 8pm.

The main **tourist office** for Ibiza Town is opposite the Catedral in Dalt Vila (Casa de la Cúria, Pl. de la Catedral, July–Sept Mon–Sat 10am–2pm & 6–9pm, Sun 10am–2pm; April–June Mon–Sat 10am–2pm & 5–8pm, Sun 10am–2pm; Oct–March Mon–Fri 9am–3pm, Sat & Sun 10am–2pm; ☏ 971 399 232, ⓦ ibiza. travel). There's also an information point at Plaça Julià Verdera in Figueretes and an island-wide information booth next to the Formentera ferry terminal on Av. Santa Eulària.

October, however, the pace abates, most of the restaurants and bars shut up shop, and the area becomes a virtual ghost town.

Passeig Marítim

MAP P.31, POCKET MAP B6–D7

The best place to start exploring La Marina is at the southwestern corner of the harbourfront, along **Passeig Marítim**. Heading east, a cluster of upmarket café-bars and restaurants afford fine vistas of the yachts and docks. These venues provide an ideal standpoint for taking in the outrageous club parades that are such a feature of the Ibizan night in high season. Further along, past the Estació Marítima, the tiny **Plaça de sa Riba**, backed by tottering old whitewashed fishermen's houses, also makes an agreeable place for outdoor dining. At the very end of the *passeig*, the breakwater of Es Muro extends into the harbour and a flight of steps heads south up into Sa Penya (see below).

Plaça de sa Constitució

MAP P.31, POCKET MAP B7

This small, peaceful square of elegant whitewashed and ochre-painted old merchants' houses is home to **Es Mercat Vell** ("The Old Market"), a curiously squat Neoclassical edifice where fruit and vegetables have been traded since 1873 – today the stalls specialize in organic produce.

Sa Penya

MAP P.28, POCKET MAP D7

Sa Penya, a twisted triangle of streets hemmed in by the city walls to the south and the sea to the north, is both Ibiza's gay village and its main *gitano* (gypsy) district, home to one of the most marginalized of Spain's communities. Its crumbling facades, dark, warren-like alleys and lanes and outrageous streetlife, bars and boutiques are home to an edgy, vibrant and absorbing scene.

Calle de la Virgen

MAP P.30, POCKET MAP C7–D7

Cutting through the heart of Sa Penya, **Calle de la Virgen** (signposted as **Carrer de la Mare de Déu**) is *the* gay street in Ibiza, lined with dozens of tiny cave-like bars and restaurants, plus a fetish boutique or two. Despite its inappropriate moniker, the "Street of the Virgin" is one of the wildest on the island. An ordinary-looking, sleepy lane by day, at night it metamorphoses into a dark, urban alley dedicated to hedonism. Moving west to east, the street becomes progressively busier, narrower and more raucous, finally becoming no more than a couple of paces wide and crammed with drag queens, club dancers and perfectly honed muscle.

Carrer d'Alfons XII

MAP P.30, POCKET MAP C7–C8

During daylight hours **Carrer d'Alfons XII** is a pleasant but unremarkable corner of Sa Penya. Dotted with palm-shaded benches, it's bordered by a small octagonal building, the city's old **fish market**. By night, however, the plaza-like street is transformed into one of Ibiza's most flamboyant arenas – the final destination for the summer club parades. At around 1am, after an hour or so of posturing, the podium dancers, promoters and drag queens come together here for a final encore, which sees a surging, sociable throng spill out of some of the most stylish bars on the island.

Portal de ses Taules

MAP P.30, POCKET MAP B8

The main entrance into Dalt Vila is the appropriately imposing **Portal de ses Taules** ("Gate of the Inscriptions"). The approach alone quickens the pulse: up a mighty stone ramp, across a drawbridge

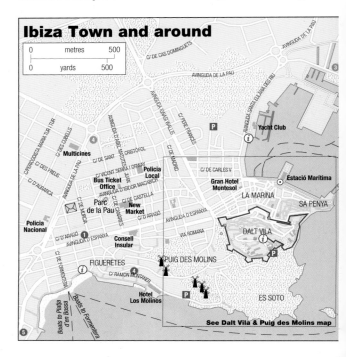

and over a dried-up moat – all part of the defences necessary to keep out sixteenth-century pirates. After passing through the gateway, you enter the old **Pati d'Armes** (armoury court), a surprisingly graceful, shady arena, while further on, graceful **Plaça de Vila** is home to an assortment of pavement cafés, restaurants, art galleries and boutiques.

Dalt Vila

Occupying a craggy peak south of the harbour, the ancient settlement of **Dalt Vila** ("High Town") is the oldest part of Ibiza Town and one of its quietest corners. The inhabitants are a disparate mix: the clergy, pockets of Ibizan high society, *gitano* families and foreigners seduced by the superb views and tranquil atmosphere. Alongside the major attractions there are a number of sights to look out for, including the walls

Dalt Vila

themselves (see p.32), and the unadorned whitewashed facade of the fifteenth-century **Església de**

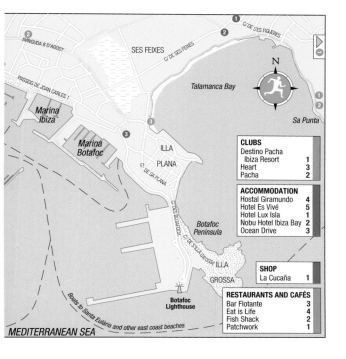

CLUBS

Destino Pacha Ibiza Resort	
Heart	3
Pacha	2

ACCOMMODATION

Hostal Giramundo	4
Hotel Es Vivé	5
Hotel Lux Isla	1
Nobu Hotel Ibiza Bay	2
Ocean Drive	3

SHOP

La Cucaña	1

RESTAURANTS AND CAFÉS

Bar Flotante	3
Eat is Life	4
Fish Shack	2
Patchwork	1

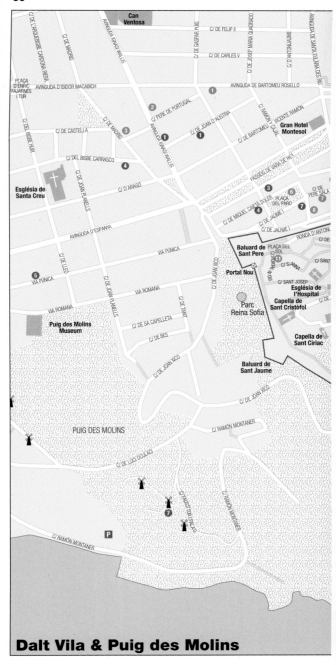

Dalt Vila & Puig des Molins

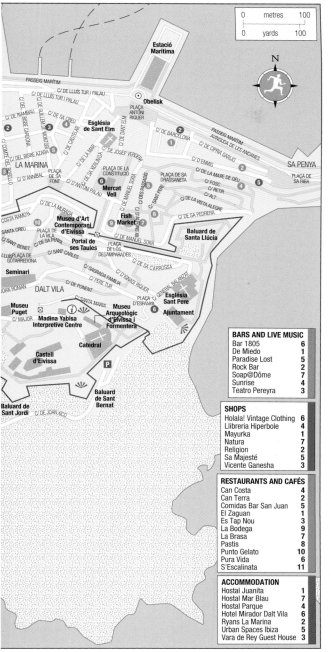

BARS AND LIVE MUSIC

Bar 1805	6
De Miedo	1
Paradise Lost	5
Rock Bar	2
Soap@Dôme	7
Sunrise	4
Teatro Pereyra	3

SHOPS

Holala! Vintage Clothing	6
Llibreria Hiperbole	4
Mayurka	1
Natura	7
Religion	2
Sa Majesté	5
Vicente Ganesha	3

RESTAURANTS AND CAFÉS

Can Costa	4
Can Terra	2
Comidas Bar San Juan	5
El Zaguan	1
Es Tap Nou	3
La Bodega	9
La Brasa	7
Pastis	8
Punto Gelato	10
Pura Vida	6
S'Escalinata	11

ACCOMMODATION

Hostal Juanita	1
Hostal Mar Blau	7
Hostal Parque	4
Hotel Mirador Dalt Vila	6
Ryans La Marina	2
Urban Spaces Ibiza	5
Vara de Rey Guest House	3

Dalt Vila's walls

Encircling the entire historic quarter of Dalt Vila, Ibiza Town's monumental Renaissance-era **walls** are the city's most distinctive structure. Completed in 1585 and still in near-perfect condition, the walls – at almost 2km long, 25m high and up to 5m thick – are some of Europe's best-preserved fortifications, and form a key part of the city's UNESCO World Heritage recognition. The Carthaginians built walls close to today's castle around the fifth century BC, and these were extended during the Moorish occupation – remnants from this period can be seen inside La Curia (see page 33) on C/ Major. Battered by centuries of attacks from pirates, the city's crumbling walls were replaced in the sixteenth century by vast new fortifications, designed by Giovanni Battista Calvi and Jacobo Fratín, which included seven colossal bastions (baluards).

l'Hospital. **Carrer Major** contains some of the grandest mansions (some bearing family coats-of-arms), the Museu Puget (see page 33), and, close to its western end, a curious chapel, the **Capella de Sant Ciriac**. Little more than a shrine in the wall protected by a metal grille, it is said to be the entrance to a secret tunnel through which the Catalans and Aragonese stormed the Moorish citadel in 1235.

Dalt Vila's historic buildings, bastions and walls provide an atmospheric backdrop to numerous events and festivals throughout the year, including the cutting-edge International Music Summit and the rambunctious three-day medieval fair – both in May (see page 8). Traditional Ibizan dancing (Ball pagès) is performed every Friday evening (July–Sept; 9.30pm; free) at the Baluard de Sant Pere, which is also host to occasional outdoor cinema screenings by candlelight (www.cinemaparadisoibiza.com). On Saturday evenings, the town hall puts on excellent dramatized tours bringing the history of Dalt Vila to life, which kids in particular will enjoy. See www.evissa.es for details.

Museu d'Art Contemporani d'Eivissa

MAP P.30, POCKET MAP B7
R. Narcís Puget s/n, Dalt Vila. 📞 971 302 723, 🌐 eivissa.es/mace/. April–June & Sept Tues–Fri 10am–2pm & 5–8pm, Sat & Sun 10am–2pm; July–Aug Tues–Fri 10am–2pm & 6–9pm, Sat & Sun 10am–2pm; Oct–March Tues–Fri 10am–4.30pm, Sat & Sun 10am–2pm. Free.

Ibiza's **Museu d'Art Contemporani** is housed in a former arsenal; the building was begun in 1727 and later used as a barracks and as the stables of the Infantry Guard. Today, its five floors house a mix of temporary and permanent modern art collections by both local and international artists, all of whom have a connection of some kind to the island. Check out the work of island-born Tur Costa and the challenging abstract art of Ibiza visitors Will Faber, Hans Hinterreiter and Erwin Broner. Also of interest are the archeological remains, some dating back to sixth century BC, that were discovered during renovations to the building in 2006 and which are now on display under a glass floor in the basement.

Museu Puget

MAP P.30, POCKET MAP A8–B8

C/ Major 18, Dalt Vila. ☎ 971 392 147.
April–June & Sept Tues–Fri 10am–2pm &
5–8pm, Sat & Sun 10am–2pm; July–Aug
Tues–Fri 10am–2pm & 6–9pm, Sat &
Sun 10am–2pm; Oct–March Tues–Fri
10am–4.30pm, Sat & Sun 10am–2pm. Free.

This museum has a large
permanent collection of paintings
and photographs by renowned
Ibizan artist **Narcís Puget Viñas**
(1874–1960), including some
superb monochrome images of
the island. The museum building,
which dates back to the fifteenth
century, is also of considerable
interest and was once one of Ibiza's
grandest mansions. Known as
Can Comasema, it boasts a fine
facade with Gothic-style windows,
a delightful central courtyard and
wonderful views of the harbour.

Museu Arqueològic d'Eivissa i Formentera

MAP P.30, POCKET MAP B8

Plaça de la Catedral. Currently closed for
renovation and excavation; due to reopen
in 2019.

The **Museu Arqueològic
d'Eivissa i Formentera** provides an overview
of Pitiusan history from prehistoric
times to the end of Islamic rule
in the thirteenth century. The
building itself is also of interest,
its simple stone facade belying a
much bigger interior and its role
as the Universitat, Ibiza's seat of
government until 1717. There's
a fine, ribbed vault roof in the
museum's entrance hall (originally
a chapel) that dates from the
fourteenth century.

Catedral

MAP P.30, POCKET MAP D4

Plaça de la Catedral. Daily June–Nov
9.30am–1.30pm & 4–7pm, Dec–May
9.30am–1.30pm & 6–9pm; services take
place on Sun at 10.30am. Free.

Dalt Vila's strategic importance is
obvious once you reach Plaça de la
Catedral, which affords magnificent
views over the port area to the

Roman amphorae in Museu Arqueològic

open ocean and Formentera. This
summit has been a place of worship
for two and a half millennia,
and the site for a succession of
ceremonial structures: Carthaginian
and Roman temples, a Moorish-
built mosque and the Gothic
Catalan cathedral that stands here
today. A former parish church,
it was granted cathedral status in
1782 and dedicated to Santa Maria
de les Neus (Mary of the Snows).
The cathedral also contains the
Museu Diocesà, which is dedicated
to religious art, and takes in a
brooding collection of religious
portraits and the odd ecclesiastical
curio, including some Renaissance
choir books.

Madina Yabisa Interpretive Centre

MAP P.30, POCKET MAP B8

Casa de la Cúria, C/ Major 2, Dalt Vila.
April–June & Sept Tues–Fri 10am–2pm &
5–8pm, Sat & Sun 10am–2pm; July–Aug
Tues–Fri 10am–2pm & 6–9pm, Sat &
Sun 10am–2pm; Oct–March Tues–Fri
10am–4.30pm, Sat & Sun 10am–2pm. €2,
children free.

Across from the catedral is
La Cúria, a late Gothic-style

courthouse that contains a tourist information desk (see page 27) and an impressive **interpretive centre** dedicated mainly to Ibiza's Muslim era, when the island was known as Yebisah. Excavated sections of medieval defensive walls are laid bare, and there are exhibits of Moorish pottery, Qu'rans and high-tech displays that offer computer-generated images and videos of life in Islamic Ibiza.

Castell d'Eivissa

MAP P.30, POCKET MAP D4

A rambling strip of buildings constructed in a fractious contest of architectural styles, **Castell d'Eivissa** squats atop the very highest ground in Dalt Vila. Construction began in the eighth century, although modifications were still being made as late as the eighteenth century. During the Spanish Civil War, the castle was the setting for one of the darkest chapters in Ibizan history, when mainland Anarchists, briefly in control of the island, massacred over a hundred Ibizan Nationalist prisoners before fleeing the island.

Castell d'Eivissa

For the best perspective of the crumbling facade, head south to the **Baluard de Sant Bernat**. From here you can make out the sixteenth-century former governor's residence – slab-fronted, dusty pink and with three iron balconies – and rising above this to the left the towers of the Almudaina, the Moorish keep. The southerly views from Sant Bernat are also spectacular, with Formentera clearly visible on the horizon and the sprawling Ibizan resorts of Figueretes and Platja d'en Bossa hugging the coastline just a couple of kilometres away.

Plaça d'Espanya

MAP P.30, POCKET MAP C8

Directly below the cathedral, **Plaça d'Espanya** is a narrow, open-ended cobbled square shaded by palm trees. The imposing arcaded building with the domed roof that dominates the plaza was originally built as a Dominican monastery in 1587, before being converted to today's **Ajuntament** (town hall). Opposite the Ajuntament is the elegant *Hotel Mirador* (see page 115), while to the rear is one of Ibiza's most handsome churches, the whitewashed sixteenth-century **Església de Sant Pere**. At the eastern end of the plaça (from where there are fine sea views) is a recumbent statue of Guillem de Montgrí, a crusading Catalan baron who helped drive the Moors from Ibiza in 1235. It's a short walk from here along the edge of the walls to the vast, five-sided **Baluard de Santa Llúcia**, the largest of the seven bastions that define the perimeters of Ibiza Town's walls.

Vara de Rey and around

MAP P.30, POCKET MAP A7

An imposing and graceful tree-lined boulevard with beautiful early twentieth-century buildings, **Vara de Rey** is the hub of modern Ibiza. It's here that you'll find one

Necropolis of Puig des Molins

of Ibiza's most famous hotel-bars, the *Gran Hotel Montesol*, and a collection of fashionable boutiques, restaurants and cafés. Smack in the middle of the avenue is a large stone-and-iron monument dedicated to Ibiza-born General Joachim Vara de Rey, who died in the Battle of Caney fought between Spain and the USA over Cuba in 1889.

Just a block to the south, the **Plaça des Parc** is an even more inviting place for a coffee or a snack, night or day, with a myriad of café-bars and restaurants grouped around a square shaded by acacias and palms. There's no traffic at all to contend with here, and the small plaça attracts an intriguing mix of stylish Ibizan denizens and bohemian characters. The bars all have plenty of atmosphere: try *Pura Vida* (see page 41) or the bar at *Hostal Parque* (see page 114).

Puig des Molins and the Necropolis

MAP P.30, POCKET MAP B3
Via Romana 31, March–Oct Tues–Sat 10am–2pm & 6–8pm, Sun 10am–2pm; Nov–Feb Tues–Sat 9am–3pm, Sun 10am–2pm. €2.40

Five minutes' walk south of Vara de Rey, **Puig des Molins** ("Hill of the Windmills") was one of the most important Punic burial sites in the Mediterranean. It was chosen by the Phoenicians in the seventh century BC because their burial requirements specified a site free from poisonous creatures – there are no snakes or scorpions on Ibiza. Noblemen were buried on this necropolis in their thousands, their bodies transported here from all over the empire.

Despite its UNESCO World Heritage status, Puig des Molins today is pretty unassuming to look at, appearing little more than a barren rocky park scattered with olive trees. However, the hillside of Puig des Molins is riddled with over three thousand tombs, and excavations over the years have unearthed some splendid terracotta figurines, amphorae and amulets; most of the finds are gathered in the museum building adjacent to the site. A short trail winds around the site enabling you to get a good look inside the burial chambers carved into the hillside. There are also some Punic artefacts at the

Cala Talamanca

Museu Arqueològic d'Eivissa i
Formentera, due to reopen in 2019
(see page 33).

Marina Botafoc

MAP P.28, POCKET MAP F2
Bus #12B from Ibiza Town, all year, daily.
Boat from Passeig Marítim, May–Oct daily.
Occupying the northern side of
Ibiza Town's bay, **Marina Botafoc**,
once part of the capital's vegetable
patch, *Ses Feixes*, is now a wealthy
enclave of yacht clubs, luxury
apartment blocks and the clubs
Heart and *Pacha* (see page 43).

Further along, beyond the
Ocean Drive hotel (see page
115), the slender, kilometre-
long Botafoc peninsula stretches
southeast into the harbour, with
a wide road running along its
length and a lighthouse defining
its final rocky extremity – cava-
swigging revellers traditionally
congregate here to witness the first
sunrise of the New Year. Beyond
the lighthouse, a new concrete
dock juts into the harbour
waters, offering photographers
an arresting perspective of the
fortress-like summit of Dalt Vila
across the waves.

Talamanca

MAP P.28, POCKET MAP F2–H2
Bus #12B from Ibiza Town, all year, daily.
Boat from Passeig Marítim, May–Oct daily.
A sweeping sandy bay 2km north
of Ibiza Town (a 30min walk via
Marina Botafoc along Passeig
de Joan Carles I), **Talamanca**
rarely gets too crowded, despite
its close proximity to the capital.
New building has been fairly
restrained here, with hotels
mainly confined to the northern
and southern fringes. Even the
presence of recent 5-star arrival
Nobu is understated (see page
115), while nearby Petit Pereyra
serves up one of Ibiza's coolest
low-key club-dining experiences.
A smattering of bars and some
good fish restaurants, including
popular *Bar Flotante* (see page
39) back the shoreline, which
is popular with families – the
gently shelving beach is ideal for
children.

Cap Martinet

POCKET MAP D13
From the northern edge of
Talamanca beach, it's possible
to continue walking east along

a coastal footpath towards Sa Punta and **Cap Martinet**. As well as offering great views back over the bay and beyond to Ibiza Town, the route passes the superb Lebanese restaurant, *Patchwork* (see page 40), the humble but excellent *Fish Shack* (see page 40), then finally swanky Pacha-run beach-club and hotel, *Destino* (see page 42), before giving way to the secluded cliffs and small, rocky bay at Cap Martinet.

S'Estanyol

POCKET MAP B12

The idyllic sandy cove of **S'Estanyol**, one of Ibiza's most isolated bays, is best approached from the town of Jesús, northwest of Talamanca. Take Carrer de S'Estanyol up past the football pitch in Jesús and, after 200m or so, you'll see a rock on the right painted 'Cala Bonita' and 'Playa S'Estanyol' indicating a turn off that takes you down a bumpy dirt track. There's a small patch of sand and plenty of rocky ledges for sunbathing, as well as the lovely beach bar and restaurant, *Cala Bonita* (open all year, except mid-Jan to end of Feb).

Figueretes

MAP P.28, POCKET MAP B4

Bus #14 from Ibiza Town, all year daily, plus hourly night buses June–Sept. Bus #36 from the airport end June to mid-Sept daily. Bus #11B from Ibiza Town (destination Ses Salines) May–Sept daily. Boat from Passeig Marítim, May–Oct daily.

The suburb-resort of **Figueretes** lies only a fifteen-minute walk southwest of the capital. Although there's a basic seaside appeal here and an attractive palm-lined promenade, the sandy beach, backed by a dense concentration of unruly apartment blocks, isn't one of the island's finest. Unlike many Ibizan resorts, there's a small resident population, and in winter, when the tourists have gone, elderly Ibizans reclaim the streets to stroll, chat and take the sea air.

Undoubtedly one of the most happening places in Ibiza during the 1950s (a collection of Dutch writers and artists spent several seasons here) and the focus of the early beatnik scene in the 1960s, there's little evidence today of Figueretes' boho past. Nightlife and eating options are plentiful but perfunctory, and the main draw is location – Figueretes makes a convenient and economic base for serious forays into the dynamic night scene just around the bay. A good selection of boat trips and activity providers also operate from here, including ferry services to Platja d'en Bossa, Ibiza Town and Formentera, as well as kayak and SUP board tours with Kayak Ibiza (W kayak-ibiza.com).

Platja de ses Figueretes

Shops

Holala! Vintage Clothing

MAP P.28, POCKET MAP B7

Pl. de la Constitució 12, Mercat Vell.
Ⓦ holala-ibiza.com. May–Oct daily 11am–
midnight.

Ibiza's first vintage clothing store
offering a wide range of men and
women's clothing, all organised
by date, from 1900–1960s. The
colourful collections of party
outfits, dance costumes, shoes
and accessories are great for a
rummage.

La Cucaña

MAP P.28, POCKET MAP B3

C/ d'Aragó 107, Ibiza Town. Ⓣ 971 303 880.
Mon–Fri 9.30am–1.30pm & 5–8.30pm, Sat
10am–1.30pm.

Ibiza's premier dressing up and
party shop, crammed with fancy
dress outfits, dance costumes,
make-up, hair accessories, party
paraphernalia and fireworks.

Llibreria Hiperbole

MAP P.28, POCKET MAP C3

C/ del Bisbe Carrasco 1–3, Ibiza Town.
Ⓣ 971 391 769, Ⓦ hiperbole.net.
Mon–Fri 9am–8.30pm, Sat 9am–2pm.

Independent book shop that
has been going for over thirty
years, specialising in classical
literature, educational resources
and languages, as well as hosting
cultural events such as poetry
slams, workshops and book
launches.

Mayurka

MAP P.28, POCKET MAP C3

Av. d'Ignasi Wallis 12, Ibiza Town. Ⓣ 971
317 653, Ⓦ mayurkaibiza.com. May–Oct
10.30am–9pm, Nov–April 10.30am–2pm
& 5–8.30pm.

Two floors of designer clothes for
women. Labels include: Valentino,
Giuseppe Zanotti, Kenzo, Stella
McCartney, Balenciaga and Chloé,
among others.

Natura

MAP P.28, POCKET MAP A7

Plaça des Parc 7, Ibiza Town. Ⓣ 971 394
328, Ⓦ naturaselection.com. June–Sept
daily 10am–11pm, Oct–May Mon–Sat
10am–9pm.

Attractive store specializing in
clothing, accessories and homeware
with an ethnic flavour, as well as
gifts, wellness products and a small
but interesting range of books and
electronic gadgets.

Religion

MAP P.28, POCKET MAP A7

C/ Comte de Rosselló, Pl. Vara de Rey.
Ⓦ religionclothingibiza.com. May–Oct
daily 10.30am–1am, Nov–April daily
10.30am–2pm & 5–8.30pm.

Unisex clothing and accessories
brand, whose distressed vintage
and rock-chic aesthetic,
complete with recurring skull
motif, makes a nice contrast
to the glitter and bling
omnipresent elsewhere.

Sa Majesté

MAP P.28, POCKET MAP D7

C/ Mare de Déu 67, Sa Penya.
Ⓦ samajesteibiza.com. Daily 6pm–2am.

Luxury erotic boutique and fetish
shop aptly located in the heart
of Ibiza's most open-minded
district. Clothes, accessories,
ornaments and toys for both men
and women, of all persuasions, are
offered with discretion, privacy
and zero judgement.

Vicente Ganesha

MAP P.28, POCKET MAP B7

C/ Guillem de Montgrí 14, La Marina. Ⓣ 660
301 549. April–Sept daily 11am–2pm &
6pm–midnight.

Famous unisex clothing shop that's
been going for over twenty years.
The interior is tightly packed with
racks of vintage and second-
hand clothes, bags, shoes and
accessories, while outside Vicente's
own ethnic-inspired collection is
on display.

Restaurants and cafés

Bar Flotante

MAP P.28, POCKET MAP F2

Platja de Talamanca ☏ 971 190 466. May–Sept daily 9am–midnight, Oct, Nov, March & April daily 9am–6pm.

Highly enjoyable, inexpensive and informal café-restaurant at the southern end of Talamanca Beach where you can dine right by the waves and watch a stream of planes swoop down towards the airport. Offers huge portions, with good fish and seafood such as hake (€11) or grilled prawns or squid (€15). Children are very welcome.

Can Costa

MAP P.28, POCKET MAP B7

C/ de sa Creu 17, La Marina. Daily 1–3.30pm & 8–11pm.

This place, in the maze of streets in the old town, serves authentic Spanish cuisine at rock-bottom prices. The daily menu (not available in high season) at €11 is both substantial and excellent value, or try one of the sumptuous bocadillos.

Can Terra

MAP P.28, POCKET MAP C3

Ignacio Wallis 14, Ibiza Town. ☏ 971 310 064, ☒ canterraibiza.com. Daily 8.30am–2am.

Superb pintxos in elegant surroundings at very reasonable prices. The pintxos are the main event (€1.65 each, serve yourself and pay by the stick, available while they last) but the menu and the Spanish wine list are also excellent. Try the grilled sirloin steak with goat's cheese sauce (€14.35) with a glass of Rioja (from €1.65 by the glass).

Comidas Bar San Juan

MAP P.28, POCKET MAP B7

C/ G. de Montgri 8, La Marina. ☏ 971 311 603. Mon–Sat 1–3.30pm & 8.30–11pm.

Venerable restaurant that's been run by the same hospitable family for

Can Terra

generations. Two tiny, atmospheric wood-panelled rooms and tasty, inexpensive Spanish and Ibizan dishes: paella, calamari, gambas, etc, for around €10 a head. You may be asked to share a table, particularly in high season.

Eat is Life

MAP P.28, POCKET MAP B2

Av. de la Pau 1, Ibiza Town. ☏ 971 312 201, ☒ eatislife.es. Mon–Sat 8.30am–8.30pm.

Healthy fast-food restaurant and café, plus mini organic shop, serving a popular lunchtime buffet (1–4.30pm, 3 dishes €11.90, 2 dishes €9). The menu changes daily but ingredients are always healthy and organic, with plenty of vegetarian options, including quiche, gazpacho, salads and tofu. Outside buffet times, simple dishes and take away boxes are available. Slightly out of town on the main ring road, but the quality and variety are worth the trip.

El Zaguan

MAP P.28, POCKET MAP C3

C/ Bartolomé Roselló 15, Ibiza Town. ☒ elzaguan.es. May–Oct 12.30pm–11.30pm, Nov–April 12.30pm–12.30am.

The decor is not glamorous but locals flock here for excellent, authentic tapas, pintxos and raciones at good value prices, such as octopus a feira, patatas bravas or beef chops. Reservations not possible.

La Brasa

In a wonderful setting overlooking the walls of Dalt Vila, this old warehouse has been stylishly converted blending historic architecture with eclectic, bohemian decor. It's a fun, buzzy place to kick off an evening with tapas (from €4–6) and cocktails (from €8).

La Brasa

MAP P.28, POCKET MAP A7

C/ Pere Sala 3, Ibiza Town. ☎ 971 301 202, Ⓦ labrasaibiza.com. Daily 11am–1am.

Classy restaurant with a delightful garden terrace shaded by plants and palm trees, and an attractive interior (where a log fire burns in winter). The innovative menu concentrates on Mediterranean fish and grilled meat. It's a good place to splash out, particularly on the grilled lobster (€39.50).

Es Tap Nou

MAP p.28, POCKET MAP C3

C/ de Madrid 18, Ibiza Town. ☎ 971 399 841. Mon–Sat 7.30am–10.30pm.

Lively juice and salad bar attached to a fruit & veg shop a 5min walk from Vara de Rey. The mouth-watering juices range from fresh orange (€2.50) to pineapple, papaya and mango (€4.55). Also serves salads (from €6), tostadas and bocatas (€1.50–4) and takeaways.

Fish Shack

MAP P.28, POCKET MAP H2

Sa Punta, Talamanca. Daily except Wed & Thurs, 11am–11pm.

Humble shack on the beach serving superb fresh fish. With no telephone number or website, reservations are not possible and there's no menu either, only the freshest fish available from the market that morning is served. If available, try the sword fish fillet (€23.50) or the prawns (€26.50). Everything is cooked on the grill with olive oil and garlic, and served with salad.

La Bodega

MAP P.28, POCKET MAP B7

C/ Bisbe Torres Mayans 2. ☎ 971 192 740, Ⓦ labodegaibiza.es. Daily 6pm–late.

Pastis

MAP P.28, POCKET MAP A7

C/ d'Avicenna 2, Pl. des Parc. ☎ 971 391 999, Ⓦ pastisibiza.com. Mon–Thurs 8.30pm–1am, Fri & Sat 8.30pm–1.30am.

Superb restaurant – the choice of Ibiza chefs – serving mainly French cuisine, such as steak tartare 'maître d'hôtel' (€35) or escargots de Bourgone Farcis (€31), as well as a handful of Spanish and international specialities, including *chuletón*, suckling pig and ceviche. Their French and Spanish wine list is extensive, as is their mouth-watering specials board.

Patchwork

MAP P.28, POCKET MAP H2

Rooftop of Sa Punta, Es Puet de Talamanca ☎ 971 193 424, Ⓦ sapuntaibiza.com. May–Sept daily 7pm–2am.

Sa Punta is home to three restaurants and *Patchwork* – to date the only Lebanese restaurant in Ibiza – occupies the building's beautiful rooftop terrace. Seating is at elegant white tables adorned with patch-worked cushions and quilts, which are lit up at night by colourful candles and lamps. Dishes are designed to share and include hot and cold meze, salads and kebabs, with good vegetarian options available. Highly recommended.

Punto Gelato

MAP P.28, POCKET MAP B7

Pl. Vila 7, Dalt Vila ☎ 606 805 650. April, May & Oct daily 10am–1am, June–Sept daily 10am–2am.

Tucked away in an easy-to-miss spot around the corner from the Museu d'Art Contemporani, this diminutive establishment serves up some of the best ice cream and sorbet in Ibiza – try the raspberry, mango or tiramisu. Scopes are served in cones or cups (small €3, medium €4, large €5) to take away or enjoy at one of the patio tables.

Pura Vida

MAP P.28, POCKET MAP A7

Plaça des Parc 2, Ibiza Town. May–Sept Mon–Sat 10.30am–4am, Sun 6pm–3.30am; Oct–April daily 10am–2am.

Perhaps the pick of the cafés on pretty Plaça des Parc, *Pura Vida* is simple and stylish and attracts a disparate clientele. Serving sandwiches and bagels from €5, tapas, such as tortilla de patatas for €5.80, as well as fresh juices and sangria.

S'Escalinata

MAP P.28, POCKET MAP A8

C/ des Portal Nous 10, Dalt Vila. ☎ 971 306 193, ⓦ sescalinata.es. Easter–Oct daily 11am–3am.

With a tiny interior, the focus of this bar/café are the large colourful cushions and low tables placed on the steps outside. With great views over Ibiza Town, a thoughtful salad, sandwich and tapas menu, and a wide range of gin (€11) and speciality cocktails (€12).

Bars and live music

Bar 1805

MAP P.28, POCKET MAP C7

C/ Santa Lucía 7, Sa Penya ☎ 651 625

972, ⓦ bar1805ibiza.com. April–Sept daily 8pm–3.30am, Oct to mid-Dec Wed–Sat 8pm–3am.

French bistro famed for its Absinthe cocktails, including the signature Green Beast, served up by Ibiza visionary and cocktail maestro, Charles Vexenat, to a backdrop of electro-swing, rock and jazz.

De Miedo

MAP P.28, POCKET MAP C7

C/ la Trinitat 6, La Marina. ☎ 603 472 317, ⓦ facebook.com/rockibizademiedo/. June–Oct daily 10pm–4am, Nov–May Thurs–Sat 10pm–4am.

Appropriately dark and grungy rock bar, tucked away down a quiet street off busy C/ Barcelona in La Marina. Going for well over 20 years, it has a large interior and a stage area that's host to regular live music events and jam sessions. See Facebook page for event details.

Paradise Lost

MAP P.28, POCKET MAP C7

C/ del Passadís 14, Sa Penya. ☎ 627 589 205, ⓦ facebook.com/paradiselostibiza/. May–Sept daily 9pm–3.30am, Oct–Dec & March–April Thurs–Sat 9pm–3.30am.

Patchwork

S'Escalinata

Soap@Dôme

MAP P.28, POCKET MAP C7
C /d'Alfons XII 5, Sa Penya. ☎ 695 957 402.
May–Oct daily 10pm–4am.

Gay Ibiza at its most gorgeous: stunning bar staff, horrifically expensive drinks and an ideal location, in the plaza-like environs of C/ d'Alfons XII. As the final destination of most of the club parades, the atmosphere on the terrace reaches fever pitch by 1am during the summer, when it's filled with a riotous assemblage of hipsters, wannabes and drag queens.

Sunrise

MAP P.28, POCKET MAP C7
C/ de la Mare de Déu 44, Sa Penya. ☎ 677 489 827. May–Oct daily 10pm–4am.

Popular and stylish bar, though nothing gets going until around midnight. It's dubbed the only lesbian bar in town but actually attracts a mixed clientele. Run by a party-hard crowd, the mojitos here are superb.

Teatro Pereyra

MAP P.28, POCKET MAP B7
C/ Comte Rosselló 3, Ibiza Town. ☎ 971 304 432, ⓦ teatropereyra.com. Mon–Sat 9am–5am.

Set in what was the foyer of a fine nineteenth-century theatre, this is Ibiza Town's premier live-music venue. There's a lively bar and a superb calendar of blues, reggae, rock and jazz acts. Free entry, but drinks triple in price when the live music starts at midnight. By day, it's a stylish café ideal for a tapa or two and a beer.

Clubs

Destino Pacha Ibiza Resort

MAP P.28, POCKET MAP H1
C/ Arrapatxitas 2, Cap Martinet s/n. ☎ 971 971 317 411 ⓦ destinoibiza.com. May to mid-Oct.

Beach-club and hotel-resort that ticks all the boxes: gorgeous

Cool little bar, with an optimal people-watching terrace overlooking C/ del Passadís in Sa Penya. Inside, vintage style chesterfield sofas, art deco palms, fairy lights and other nick nacks and eccentricities cram together to make a delightfully oddball place to enjoy their specialty rum cocktails (€12) and fine music. Open all year, it's very popular with locals and residents who make up most of the clientele. See Facebook page for DJ listings and events.

Rock Bar

MAP P.28, POCKET MAP C7
C/ Cipriano Garijo 14, La Marina. May–Oct daily noon–3.30am.

This British-run island institution is a second home for a crowd of characterful expats and pre-clubbers. Staff are friendly and you're guaranteed to meet fellow fun-seekers. The owners have good connections to all the clubs (so free passes are sometimes available) and the capacious terrace is one of the prime places to enjoy Ibiza's long Balearic nights.

Hitting the clubs

Clubs cost around €25–60 to get in and are open between midnight and 6am – try to blag a guest pass from one of the bars on the harbour front. The Discobus (end of May– beginning of Oct, midnight–7am; €3–4, ⓦ discobusibiza.com, see page 123) ferries partygoers from Ibiza Town to the island's major clubs, leaving from the main port. The highly recommended website ⓦ **ibizaspotlight.com** has a party calendar and full details of club nights, events and tickets.

pool area decked with Bali beds, hammocks, palm trees and a cocktail bar; a sea-view restaurant; plus an Ushuaia-style stage area hosting parties, events and club nights (usually Thurs & Sun, free for hotel guests, €40–60 general public, see website for details). Beautifully done but your wallet will certainly know it's been Destinoed.

Heart

MAP P.28, POCKET MAP E1
Passeig Joan Carles 1, 17, Marina Botafoc. ⓘ **971 933 777** ⓦ **heartibiza.com.** May–Oct.
A complete sensory experience mixing fine dining, performance art, live bands and electronic music, from the founder and creator of Cirque du Soleil, Guy Laliberté, and his friends, the renowned Spanish chefs, brothers Ferran and Albert Adrià, of elBulli fame. Reservation for dinner is essential, and prices are not cheap, but they include the jaw-dropping shows as well as entry to the themed party nights that follow on from 1.30–6am. Club nights, such as popular Boogie in Wonderland and La Troya, don't require pre-booking and tend to attract a younger crowd.

Pacha

MAP P.28, POCKET MAP E1
Av. 8 d'Agost 27, Marina Botafoc. ⓦ **pacha. com.** Daily April–Oct, Oct–March weekends only.
Most Ibizans rate *Pacha* in a class of its own; indeed when referring to the club the answer is simply "*Pacha es Pacha*". A global empire – over seventy *Pacha*s are dotted around the world, from Marrakesh to Buenos Aires – centred in Ibiza, the island remains HQ for a dance franchise founded on chic, Balearic-style clubbing, with visits from the world's top DJS including Pete Tong and Solomun (entry €40–80).

The club itself has a capacity of around 3000, built in a series of terraces that betray its origins as a farmhouse, and the whitewashed exterior of the old *finca*, framed by floodlit palm trees, creates a real sense of occasion. Classy little details are everywhere, with Spanish tiles evoking a Mediterranean theme, while the elegant terrace, spread over several layers, is a wonderfully sociable, open-air affair, with vistas of the city skyline.

Pacha

The east

Ibiza's indented eastern coastline is dotted with family-oriented resorts and sheltered coves. Many of the sandy beaches, such as Cala Llonga and Cala de Sant Vicent, were developed decades ago into bucket-and-spade holiday enclaves, but plenty of undeveloped bays remain, such as Cala Mastella, the cliff-backed cove of Cala Boix and the unspoilt sands of Aigües Blanques. Santa Eulària des Riu, the region's municipal capital, is a pleasant town that acts as a focus for the east coast's resorts and has a friendly, familial appeal as well as a lively restaurant strip, two beaches and a marina. Further north lie pretty Sant Carles and the hamlet of Sant Vicent, surrounded by some of Ibiza's most spectacular scenery: forested hillsides, sweeping valleys and rugged coves.

Cala Llonga

MAP P.45, POCKET MAP D12
Bus #15 from Ibiza Town, May–Oct daily, Nov–April Mon–Fri. Bus #41 from Santa Eulària, May–Oct daily, Nov–April Mon–Fri. Boats from Santa Eulària & Formentera, May–Oct daily.

Heading north from Ibiza Town, the first of the *calas* (coves) on the east coast is the family resort of **Cala Llonga**. Set in a pretty inlet, the wide bay has fine, gently shelving sand and usually calm, translucent water. There are full beachside facilities and a tourist information kiosk (May–Oct Mon–Sat 10am–2pm). As in many Ibizan resorts, the cuisine on offer is a little uninspiring, with *Can Nuts* (tapas) or *El Deseo* (Mexican) both on C/ des Munt Aconcagua the best bets. From Cala Llonga, it's a short drive to Sol d'en Serra, an unremarkable pebble beach except for the stunning restaurant and beach club, *Amante*, built into the cliffs behind (see page 52).

Santa Eulària

MAP P.46, POCKET MAP D12
Bus #13 from Ibiza Town, daily. Bus #19 from Sant Antoni, April–Nov Mon–Sat. Bus #24 from airport, Jun–Oct daily. Boat from Ibiza Town, May–Oct daily.

Arrival and information

Getting around the east on public transport is fairly easy. Santa Eulària is served by frequent **buses** from Ibiza Town and is well connected to the area's resorts and villages by regular bus and **boat** services (indicated in the text). However, to get to the more remote beaches, you'll need your own transport.

Santa Eulària's bus station is on Camí de Missa, a couple of blocks north of the Plaça d'Espanya. Boats leave from a dock on the west side of the Marina. From May to the end of October, they serve Formentera, Ibiza Town and beaches to the north and south, see ⓦ santaeulaliaferry.com for more details. There's a tourist information centre (☏ 971 330 728, ⓦ visitsantaeulalia.com) on C/ Marià Riquer Wallis 4.

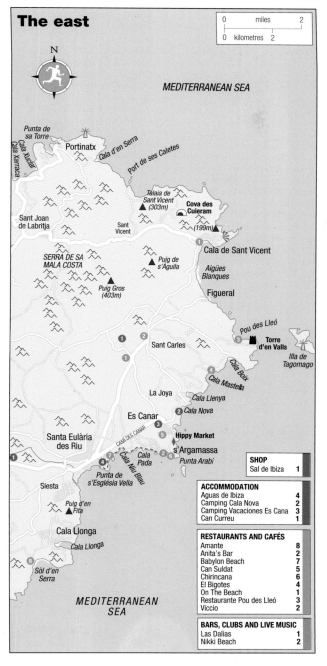

The east

MEDITERRANEAN SEA

Punta de
sa Torre
Cala Xuclar
Cala Xarraca
Portinatx
Cala d'en Serra
Port de ses Caletes

Talaia de
Sant Vicent
(303m)
**Cova des
Cuieram**
(199m)

Cala de Sant Vicent

Sant Joan
de Labritja

Sant
Vicent

*SERRA DE SA
MALA COSTA*

Puig de
s'Aguila

Aigües
Blanques

Figueral

Puig Gros
(403m)

Pou des Lleó

3

**Torre
d'en Valls**

Sant Carles

Illa de
Tagomago

4

Cala Boix

La Joya

Cala Mastella

Cala Llenya

2 Cala Nova

Es Canar

3

CAMÍ DES CANAR

5

Hippy Market

s'Argamassa

Santa Eulària
des Riu

6

1

7

4

Cala
Pada

2

Punta Arabí

Cala Niu Blau

Cala
Pada

Punta de
s'Església Vella

Siesta

Puig d'en
Fita

Cala Llonga

Cala Llonga

8

Sòl d'en
Serra

MEDITERRANEAN
SEA

	miles	2
0	kilometres 2	

N

SHOP

Sal de Ibiza	1

ACCOMMODATION

Aguas de Ibiza	4
Camping Cala Nova	2
Camping Vacaciones Es Cana	3
Can Curreu	1

RESTAURANTS AND CAFÉS

Amante	8
Anita's Bar	2
Babylon Beach	7
Can Suldat	5
Chirincana	6
El Bigotes	4
On The Beach	1
Restaurante Pou des Lleó	3
Viccio	2

BARS, CLUBS AND LIVE MUSIC

Las Dalias	1
Nikki Beach	2

In an island of excess, **Santa Eulària**, Ibiza's third largest town, is remarkable for its ordinariness. Understated and provincial, the town lies on the eastern bank of the only river in the Balearics. Its best aspect, however, is its shoreline; the two town **beaches** are clean and tidy, with softly sloping sands that are ideal for children, while the Marina is a popular place for a drink or meal, with plenty of choice. The graceful **Ajuntament** (town hall) dominates the north side of Plaça d'Espanya. Just below, **Passeig de s'Alamera** is easily Santa Eulària's most attractive thoroughfare, with a shady, tree-lined pedestrianized centre. On summer evenings, dozens of market stalls add a splash of colour here, selling jewellery, sarongs and the like. There's a good selection of moderately priced restaurants on C/ Sant Vicent, although nightlife is generally pretty tame.

Museu Etnogràfic d'Eivissa

MAP P.46

Av. del Pare Guasch. ☎ 971 332 845. April–Sept Mon–Sat 10am–2pm & 5.30–8pm, Sun 11am–1.30pm; Oct–March Tues–Sat 10am–2pm & Sun 11am–1.30pm. €3.

Halfway up the small hill of Puig de Missa, the **Museu Etnogràfic** has displays based on Pitiusan rural traditions. The main draw is the museum building itself, a classic example of the traditional flat-roofed Ibizan *casament* house. You enter via the *porxet* (outdoor terrace), while the cool, beamed *porxo* (long room) that now houses the ticket office would have been the heart of the household for most of the year, where corn was husked, tools sharpened and *festeig* (courting rituals) held. Exhibits include carpentry tools, musical instruments and clothing, as well as a grape press and a huge old olive-oil press.

Santa Eulària

| 0 | metres | 200 |
| 0 | yards | 200 |

Market
Bus station
Església de Puig de Missa
Cemetery
Ajuntament
Museu Etnogràfic d'Eivissa
PLAÇA D'ESPANYA
Taxis
Club Nàutic
Platja de Santa Eulària
Santa Eulària Ferry
Marina
Platja des Pins
Boats to Cala Llonga & Ibiza Town
Boats to Formentera
Boats to Cala d'Hort & Es Canar

MEDITERRANEAN SEA

| CLUB | |
| Guaraná | 1 |

| ACCOMMODATION | |
| Ca's Català | 1 |

RESTAURANTS AND CAFÉS	
Project Social	2
Taco Paco	1

Església de Puig de Missa

Església de Puig de Missa

MAP P.46
May–Oct daily 10am–2pm.
Puig de Missa's 52-metre summit
is dominated by the sculpted
lines of Santa Eulària's very fine
fortress-church, **Església de Puig
de Missa**, a white rectangular
building constructed – after pirates
destroyed the original chapel – by
the Italian architect Calvi, who
was also responsible for the walls
of Dalt Vila (see page 32).
The church's eastern flank has a
semicircular tower, dating from
1568, that formed part of Ibiza's
coastal defences. Around 1700, the
church's best feature was added: a
magnificent and wonderfully cool
porch with eight arches and mighty
pillars supporting a precarious-
looking beamed roof.

Es Canar

MAP P.45, POCKET MAP E12
**Bus #18A (all year) or #18B (June–Oct)
from Santa Eulària, daily. Bus #24 from
airport, June–Oct daily. Boats from Santa
Eulària and Ibiza Town, May–Oct daily.**
The compact resort of **Es Canar**
lies 5km northeast of **Santa
Eulària**. The inviting Blue Flag

beach, with a crescent of pale sand,
is its main attraction, offering
safe swimming and a variety of
watersports. Unfortunately, the
accompanying British-style pubs
and fast-food joints present a less
attractive picture, though the
special menus and happy hours at
least keep things economical.

It's generally a family-oriented
place and children are well catered
for. A tourist train makes trips
from here to Portinatx (see page
57) and children will also enjoy
Acrobosc (ⓦacroboscibiza.com),
assault courses and zip lines of
varying difficulty built among
the pine forest near Cala Pada.
However, it's the vast weekly hippy
market (May–Oct Wed only,
10am–6pm), held just south of the
centre in the grounds of the Club
Punta Arabí resort, that draws most
people to this part of the coast.

Cala Nova

MAP P.45
**Bus #24 from airport, June–Oct daily. Bus
#18B from Santa Eulària, June–Oct daily.
Parking at Cala Nova is free but limited.**
A kilometre north of Es Canar,
around the rocky coastline, the

Coastal walk to Punta Arabí

From the seafront promenade in Santa Eulària, an attractive, easy-to-follow coastal path follows the shoreline northeast to the modern resort of Es Canar. The 6km walk should take two or three hours, with plenty of opportunities for a swim along the way. Head east along the promenade and after about fifteen minutes you'll reach the rocky promontory of **Punta de s'Església Vella**. The path loops around the angular modernist Palau de Congressos and passes Babylon Beach (see page 52) before reaching quiet **Cala Niu Blau**, where there's a hundred-metre arc of fine, sunbed-strewn sand and a couple of simple fish restaurants.

Continuing along the coast path, past a cluster of pricey-looking villas, you'll arrive at **Cala Pada** in about thirty minutes; the 200m of fine, pale sand and shallow water here is popular with families, and there are a couple of café-restaurants. It's also a surprisingly well-connected beach, with regular **boats** to Santa Eulària and Ibiza Town during the summer, as well as excursions to Formentera (🌐 santaeulaliaferry.com).

Some 500m beyond Cala Pada, the path skirts **s'Argamassa**, a compact, fairly upmarket family resort dominated by ME Hotel and Nikki Beach club before reaching pretty Cala Martina and Chirincana beyond (see page 53). From here the path heads inland, bypassing the wooded promontory of **Punta Arabí**, which juts into the Mediterranean opposite two tiny rocky islets. It's then a ten-minute stroll into **Es Canar** (see page 47), passing the *Club Arabí* resort, where Ibiza's biggest hippy market is held. Bus #18A or B will drop you back at Santa Eulària from Es Canar.

wide, sandy bay of **Cala Nova** is one of Ibiza's most exposed beaches; its invigorating, churning waves are especially strong when there's a northerly wind blowing. Nevertheless, it gets very busy in summer, thanks in part to *Atzaró Beach*, an attractive bar-restaurant overlooking the bay that offers sumptuous seafood and cocktails. *Atzaró* also run a chiriniguito on the beach serving simple burgers and snacks.

Sant Carles

MAP P.45, POCKET MAP E11
Bus #16, 16A or 16C from Santa Eulària, daily.

Of all Ibiza's villages, the pretty, whitewashed settlement of **Sant Carles**, 7km northeast of Santa Eulària, is probably the one most steeped in hippy history.

Beatnik travellers started arriving in the 1960s, attracted by vacant farmhouses in the surrounding unspoilt countryside; the village, and specifically *Anita's Bar*, became the focus of a lively scene. *Anita's* remains open (see page 52), though these days *Las Dalias* (see page 55), nearby, is much more of a boho hangout – over the summer it's host to night markets and music events, such as the legendary Acid Sundays, making it sleepy east Ibiza's liveliest venue by far.

Cala Llenya

MAP P.45
Bus #16A from Santa Eulària, May–Oct Mon–Sat.

Southeast of Sant Carles, a signposted road weaves 4km downhill through small terraced fields of olive and carob trees before reaching **Cala Llenya**, a two-hundred-metre-wide bite-shaped sandy bay. The low sandstone cliffs are scattered with white-painted villas but, with few big hotels nearby, the fine sands never get too crowded, and a friendly beachside café (May–Oct) sells snacks and drinks.

Cala Mastella

MAP P.45

Heading north along the coast, the next beach is **Cala Mastella**, some 3km from Cala Llenya; the road descends to the shore via an idyllic terraced valley. Barely forty metres wide, the sandy beach is lovely, set at the back of a deep coastal inlet with pine trees almost touching the sheltered, emerald waters. It's an exceptionally inviting place for a swim, although watch out for sea urchins, some of which are fairly close to the shore. A kiosk (Easter–Oct) sells drinks and snacks (hamburgers and pizzas from €9, jug of cava sangria €20), but for a fine seafood lunch, walk 350m around the rocks to the north side of the bay and the *El Bigotes* restaurant (reservations essential, see page 53).

Cala Boix

MAP P.45

North of Cala Mastella, a wonderfully scenic coastal road meanders for 1km or so through pine forest, affording panoramic views over the Mediterranean below, before reaching **Cala Boix**, set below high, crumbling cliffs. It's a beautiful sliver of a beach, with coarse, darkish sand and pebbles. Three simple restaurants line the headland high above the shore – *La Noria* commands the best views – and there's a simple kiosko just above the sands for snacks and drinks.

Pou des Lleó

MAP P.45

Inland of Cala Boix, a lone country road cuts northwest for 1km or so, past large terraced fields separated by honey-coloured dry-stone walls, until you come to a signposted

Pou des Lleó

junction for the diminutive bay of **Pou des Lleó**. A tiny, pebble-and-sand-strewn horseshoe-shaped inlet, surrounded by low-lying, rust-red cliffs and lined with fishing huts, the only facilities here are a small *chiringuito* (beach café bar) on the beach (May–Oct daily 10.30am–10pm) serving simple baguettes and burgers, and the decent seafood *Restaurante Pou des Lleó* (see page 54).

Torre d'en Valls

MAP P.45

A further kilometre east towards the coast from Pou des Lleó is a seventeenth-century defence tower, **Torre d'en Valls**, set atop one of the few outcrops of volcanic rock in Ibiza. The tower is in fine condition and has metal rungs ascending its exterior wall; its door is kept locked, however. There are panoramic views over the ocean from here, towards the humpbacked island of Tagomago.

Figueral

MAP P.45, POCKET MAP E11

Bus #16C from Santa Eulària, June–Oct Mon–Sat. Boats from Ibiza Town, Santa

Eulària & Formentera May–Oct Mon–Fri. Continuing northeast, the next resort is the small and prosperous resort of **Figueral**. The narrow, two-hundred-metre stretch of exposed sand is swept clean by churning waves, but swimming conditions can get a little rough when the prevailing northeasterly blows. It hosts a clump of hotels and restaurants, the highlight of which is the *Las Dalias Chiringuito* overlooking the beach and offering paella, salads and fresh fish as well as Asian-influenced dishes and occasional live music. Kayak Ibiza (see page 126) also have a base here providing kayak and SUP rental, as well as guided tours around the island.

Aigües Blanques

MAP P.45

Bus #16C from Santa Eulària, June–Oct Mon–Sat. Car park €3.

Aigües Blanques, or "White Waters", is separated from Figueral's slender sands by a short section of eroded, storm-battered cliffs. It's accessed from the coastal road towards Cala de Sant Vicent. The 300m long slice

Torre d'en Valls

of dark sand, interspersed with rocky outcrops and crumbling cliffs and buffeted by the ocean, is relatively quiet and popular with nudists, although the height of the surrounding cliffs means it gets shady relatively early in the afternoon. Access to the beach is via a steep 200m footpath from the car park and not suitable for those with reduced mobility. The solitary *chiringuito* (Feb–Oct daily 9am–7.30pm) serves fish and homemade pizza, as well as smoothies, juices and drinks.

Cala de Sant Vicent

MAP P.45, POCKET MAP E11
Bus #16C from Santa Eulària, Jun–Oct Mon–Sat. Bus #20B from Sant Joan all year Mon–Fri.

Ibiza's isolated northeastern tip offers some of the island's most dramatic highland country, dominated by the plunging valley of Sant Vicent, west of the resort of **Cala de Sant Vicent**, the only tourist development in this near-pristine area. Getting there is an attraction in itself: driving the coastal road north of Aigües Blanques is an exhilarating experience, following the corrugated coastline and weaving through thick pine forests, with sparkling waters offshore. Three kilometres after Aigües Blanques you catch a glimpse of Cala de Sant Vicent, its sweeping arc of golden sand enclosed by the peaks to the north and steep cliffs to the south. Unfortunately, property developers have filled the shoreline with a row of ugly concrete hotels, but the waters here still offer some of the best swimming in the area.

Cova des Cuieram

MAP P.45
May–Oct Tues–Sun 9.30am–1.30pm. Free.
A kilometre inland from Cala de Sant Vicent, there's a paved turn-off on the right (north) to the **Cova des Cuieram**, an important

Cova des Cuieram

site of worship in Carthaginian times and one of the most remote spots in Ibiza. Hundreds of terracotta images of the fertility goddess Tanit have been unearthed here, some of which are now displayed in the Museu Arquelògic in Ibiza Town (see page 33). Inside, there's very little to see, though it's thought the stalactites could have been part of the cult of worship.

Port de ses Caletes

MAP P.45
A tiny pebbly cove, barely 50m across, **Port de ses Caletes** is reachable only along a tortuous (but signposted) road from Sant Vicent that ascends via switchbacks to 250m and then plummets to the sea; it's a bumpy fifteen-minute drive from the village. With a ramshackle collection of dilapidated fishing huts as its only buildings, the cove is dwarfed by soaring coastal cliffs, and it's a blissfully peaceful spot, where there's nothing much to do except listen to the waves wash over the smooth stones on the shore or snorkel round the rocky edges of the bay.

Shop

Sal de Ibiza

MAP P.45

Ctra. Sant Eulària km 3.4. ⓦ saldeibiza.
com. Mid-April to Oct daily 10am–9pm,
9.30pm in July & Aug.
Well-established brand selling
beautifully packaged table salt
products harvested exclusively
from the Ses Salines nature reserve.
This flagship Santa Eulària store
also sells other Ibizan products,
such as chocolates, olive oil and
coffee, making it a useful one-
stop-shop for stockpiling gifts and
souvenirs.

Restaurants and cafés

Amante

MAP P.45

Sol d'en Serra (near Cala Llonga). ☎ 971
196 176, ⓦ amanteibiza.com. April–Oct
daily 11am–2am.
Stunning beach restaurant built
into the cliff face at Sol d'en Serra.
Holidays could start and end at

Amante; all the elements are here:
views, sea, sand and fabulous food.
Try the monkfish, king prawns and
squid served with 'sofrito' marinero
(€28) and the homemade lemon
meringue pie (€8.50). Lots of the
veg comes from their own organic
garden and there are plenty of
options for veggies.

Anita's Bar

MAP P.45

Sant Carles, on the main through road.
☎ 971 335 090. Daily 7.30am–1.30am.
A milestone in Ibiza's bohemian
past, this vine-shaded patio
café-restaurant remains a popular
meeting point and has an
inexpensive menu of burgers,
pizzas, tapas and a good range of
drinks, including its own famous
hierbas liqueur (full meals under
€15 a head). The art on the walls
allegedly dates from the times
when 1960s artists donated
their works in exchange for
sustenance.

Babylon Beach

MAP P.45

C/Bartomeu Tur Clapés 20, Santa Eulària.
☎ 971 332 181, ⓦ babylonbeachbar.com.

Anita's Bar

May–end Oct, daily 10am–8pm.
One of the nicest beach bars in eastern Ibiza. Tables, loungers and bean bags overlook crystal clear waters, the menu focuses on local, organic produce and the bread is homemade on site. Firm favourites include the fried Caribbean chicken with mango and cashew nuts (€22) and the Babylon cheese burger (€20). There's also a beach-shack bar, kayaks, a pontoon into the sea and a play area for kids.

Can Suldat

MAP P.45

C/ Font des Murtar 44, Es Canar. ☎ 971 312 224. Open all year except Nov, Tues–Sat 8pm–3am.

Beautifully converted finca lit up at night with lamps and candles to create a wonderfully atmospheric garden restaurant, with cosy tables inside for cooler evenings. The menu is French-Suisse (fondue for two €25, raclette €9) and there's live music most nights too; mainly rock and reggae from the 60s/70s/80s.

Chirincana

MAP P.45

Av. Punta Arabí s/n, Cala Martina. ⓦ chirincana-ibiza.com. May & Oct daily 10am–1am, June–Sept 9am–1am.

Beach-shack pizza restaurant in a great location on the water's edge at Punta Arabí. There's a hippy vibe though this is not reflected in the prices (pizzas from €13) and the staff can be grisly, but there's a good range for vegetarians (try the Chirincana with goat's cheese, rocket and honey) and around sunset it turns into one of east coast Ibiza's liveliest venues with DJs, dancing, flame throwing and the like. Wed night in particular is party night, see Facebook for details.

El Bigotes

MAP P.45

Cala Mastella. ☎ 650 797 633. Easter–end

El Bigotes

Oct daily noon–6pm.

With wooden tables set right by the water's edge, this delightful lunch-only place is one of the most idyllic spots to eat in Ibiza – it's just out of sight from the beach, around the rocks on the north side of the cove. Food is served in two seatings: a mixed grilled fish platter (€18) is served at noon and *bullit de peix* (€23) at 2pm, with only drinks, coffee and dessert available from 4pm onwards. Its popularity mean it's essential to book in advance, up to a month in July & August, and it's wise to call and confirm on the day as well (between 11am–1pm).

On The Beach

MAP P.45

Cala de Sant Vicent. ☎ 971 320 115, ⓦ facebook.com/onthebeachibiza/. May, June & Sept daily 10am–1am, July & Aug daily 10am–2am.

Surf-themed restaurant crammed with surf boards, tropical plants and colourful beach nick nacks of all kinds. Famous for its burgers such as the Superman: organic beef, bacon egg and cheese (€13.50), or the spicier

Project Social

Speedy Gonzalez with guacamole, jalapeño and sour cream (€14.50). In the evenings, tables are pushed back and DJs, live music, salsa and reggae bands turn it into a lively beach club.

Project Social

MAP P.46
C/ Sant Llorenç 22, Santa Eulària. ☎ 871 110 893, ⓦ projectsocial.co. Daily 10am–1am.
Popular burger and street food restaurant with a hipster edge. Try their Tourist burger (beef patty, stilton, crispy bacon, €10.75) or the Pig & Ting (pulled pork, coleslaw, €9.50) washed down with a craft beer or a cocktail (from €8).

Restaurante Pou des Lleó

MAP P.45
Pou des Lleó s/n. ☎ 971 335 274, ⓦ poudeslleo.com. April, May & Oct daily 9am–6pm, June–Sept 9am–midnight, kitchen open 1–4pm & 7.30–10.30pm.
Modest-looking seafood restaurant perched above a tiny fishing bay in a remote spot. Serves some of the freshest fish in eastern Ibiza, including grilled lobster (€85 per

kilo) and superb paella (from €21) as well as traditional rice dishes such as *buillet de peix* (€31).

Taco Paco

MAP P.46
C/ Sant Jaume 34, Santa Eulària. ☎ 971 807 556. July–Sept Tues–Sun 7–11pm, Oct–June Wed–Sun 7–11pm.
Easy to miss in a humdrum location away from the main drag, this is arguably Santa Eulària's best restaurant. Calling itself 'Mexiterranean', it serves superb tostadas, quesadillas and tamales. Favourites include the Guacas Bravas with guacamole and chipotle sauce (€8.50) and the Passion Margarita (€8). The interior, brightly decorated with Mexican colours and shabby chic furniture, is as much fun as the food.

Viccio

MAP P.45
Ses Oliveres de Peralta 15, Sant Carles. ☎ 971 326 871, ⓦ viccio.com. April–Oct daily noon–midnight.
Premium ice creams and sorbets, made on site by the Argentinian owners using local ingredients where possible. Favourites include

the dulce de leche, with a cup or cone costing €2.50 for one scoop, €4 for two or €6 for three. They also serve delicious vegan and gluten-free lollies (try the strawberry and banana) – the sweetness provided by Ibizan dates.

Bars, clubs and live music

Las Dalias

MAP P.45
Santa Eulària–Sant Carles road km 12, Sant Carles. Ⓦ lasdalias.es. June–Sept night market & events daily except Fri 7pm–1am, see details below. April–Oct day market Sat 10am–8pm, Nov–Mar Sat 10am–6pm.

A long-standing Ibiza institution, *Las Dalias* is perhaps best described as a mini festival site hosting bars, restaurants, street food and market stalls and an eclectic clientele of tourists, hippies and locals. There's a day market on Saturdays all year round, plus a night market in summer and various weekly events: Namaste on Wednesdays is an Indian-themed night, live music and dancers, Thursdays host live concerts while Acid Sundays is as psychedelic as it sounds with guest DJs, live bands and performance artists.

Guarana

MAP P.46
Marina Santa Eulària Ⓦ guaranaibiza.com. May–Oct daily 8pm–6am; Nov–April Thurs–Sun 10.30pm–6am. Free.

Stylish and sociable, this is Santa Eulària's only club. It's got a great harbour location and showcases some live music events as well as house, electronica, funk, blues and hip hop DJs. Cocktails, such as a mai tai, Long Island Ice Tea or mojito, start from €9.

Nikki Beach

MAP P.45
Avinguda de s'Argamassa 153, S'Argamassa, ☏ 619 753 710, Ⓦ nikkibeach.com. May–Sept daily 11am–8pm.

Beach club, restaurant, pool and bar specialising in daytime parties, from champagne brunches to fiestas; drink and beach-bed packages bookable in advance.

Guarana

The northwest

From the tiny cove of Cala d'en Serra in the north to the diminutive village of Santa Agnès to the west, this is the wildest, most isolated part of Ibiza. A soaring range of towering cliffs and forested peaks, the coastline only relents to allow access to the shore in a few places. Just two bays – Port de Sant Miquel and Portinatx – have been developed for tourism. Elsewhere, the pristine and often deserted coast offers better hiking than beachlife, as well as terrific snorkelling. Inland, the thickly wooded, sparsely populated terrain is interspersed with small patches of farmland where olives, carob, almonds and citrus fruits are nourished by the rust-red earth. Only picturesque Sant Joan and sleepy Sant Miquel could realistically be described as villages, though all the other hamlets have a whitewashed church and a bar or two.

Sant Joan

MAP P.58, POCKET MAP D11
Bus #20 from Ibiza Town, May–Oct daily,
Nov–April Mon–Sat. Bus #21 from Santa
Eulària, May–Oct Mon–Sat.
High in the northern hills, the
pretty village of **Sant Joan** lies

on the main highway from Ibiza Town to Portinatx, 22km from the capital. Though only a few hundred people live here, the village is a municipal capital, boasts its own modest **Ajuntament** (town hall) and comes alive during the two

Sant Joan

Arrival and information

In summer, infrequent **buses** run to virtually every village and resort in the northwest from Ibiza Town, plus the odd service from Sant Antoni; but very few operate from Nov–Apr. Even in summer, you really need your own transport to properly explore this region, though day-trips to the likes of Sant Miquel (see page 60) and Portinatx (see page 57) are definitely feasible. Sant Joan has a friendly tourist office at C/ Alcalde Jaume Marí Roig 4 (☎ 971 333 075; June–Sept Mon–Fri 10am–2pm & 4–8pm, Sat 10am–2pm, May & Oct Mon–Sat 10am–2pm).

weekends of fiestas celebrating the Nit de Sant Joan at Midsummer (see page 130). Dominating the village skyline, the eighteenth-century church, just off the main road, has typically high, whitewashed walls and an arched side-porch.

Once an important hippy hangout, evidence of Sant Joan's countercultural leanings is somewhat muted today, though the region remains popular with a bohemian bunch of artists and writers. The spirit also survives to an extent at the Sunday Hippy Market (10am–4pm). The market stalls, clustered on the main street and on C/ Mossèn Vicent Ferrer, offer the usual mix of ethnic clothes, jewellery, scented soaps, candles and trinkets, but a lot of it is handmade and the quality is generally very good. From noon–2pm, the action turns to the little square opposite the church, where live bands play a mix of world music and blues.

Xarraca Bay

MAP P.58, POCKET MAP D10
Bus #20A from Ibiza Town, May–Oct daily, Nov–April Mon–Sat. Bus #21 from Santa Eulària, May–Oct Mon–Sat.

North of Sant Joan, the main highway to Portinatx wriggles down to the coast, following a beautiful, fertile valley flanked by olive-terraced hills and almond and citrus groves. The route affords sweeping views of the two-kilometre-long **Xarraca Bay** below, one of Ibiza's

most expansive. Dotted with tiny rocky islands, the translucent waters are backed by low cliffs, and there are three small beaches. Four kilometres along the road from Sant Joan, a signposted side-road loops past some villas to **Cala Xarraca**, a thin strip of coarse sand and pebbles no more than 150m long with a solitary bar/restaurant selling full meals and tapas.

A kilometre further along the Portinatx road, **S'Illot des Renclí** is a beautiful thirty-metre-wide patch of well-raked sand and very shallow, azure water; just offshore is the tiny islet after which the beach is named, as is the very decent fish restaurant here. A further kilometre to the east, tiny **Cala Xuclar** is a gorgeous, sandy, horseshoe-shaped inlet sprinkled with fishing huts, plus an excellent *chiringuito* (June–Sept) for meals and drinks. The beach is very tranquil and the waters offer excellent snorkelling possibilities.

Portinatx

MAP P.58, POCKET MAP D10
Bus #20A from Ibiza Town, May–Oct daily, Nov–April Mon–Sat. Bus #21 from Santa Eulària, May–Oct Mon–Sat.

Located on a double bay with three sandy beaches, its well-spaced hotels and apartment blocks set between mature pines, **Portinatx** is a friendly, family-oriented holiday centre, with a handful of decent bars and restaurants, plenty of water sports and several other good beaches nearby.

The larger of the bays, Port de Portinatx, has two attractive golden patches of sand, **S'Arenal Gross** and **S'Arenal Petite**. The other beach, **Es Portitxol** (known locally as **Playa del Puerto**), is at the end of a narrow inlet 500m west of S'Arenal Gross and has well-sheltered water, making it perfect for swimming and snorkelling; there's also a dive school here (see page 126) and the excellent *Los Enamorados* restaurant (see page 66). From Es Portitxol, it's a pretty 20-minute coastal stroll to the Portinatx lighthouse (Far des Moscarter). At the back of the beach, behind the *chiringuito*, you'll find three paths: one directly along the coast, one through the pine forest and one in between, which is the best path to take.

Things are pretty sedate for most of the year, but each July Portinatx hosts a three-day festival that includes an all-night beach party, DJs, processions, food stalls and the like.

Cala d'en Serra

MAP P.58, POCKET MAP E10

East of Portinatx, a very scenic road rises above Ibiza's northern tip, threading through woods and past isolated luxury villas. After 3km, there's a magnificent view of diminutive **Cala d'en Serra**, a remote, exquisite cove framed by green hills; it's reachable via a poor, signposted, but just about driveable dirt road. The only scar in the scenery is the ugly, half-built concrete shell of an abandoned hotel project just above the beach. The bay's alluring, translucent waters make an idyllic place for a dip, and offer rich snorkelling around the rocky fringes of the inlet; it's a short swim across to another tiny pebbly cove (also accessible over the rocks to the south). A café-shack (May–Oct) just off the beach serves decent seafood, *bocadillos* and drinks.

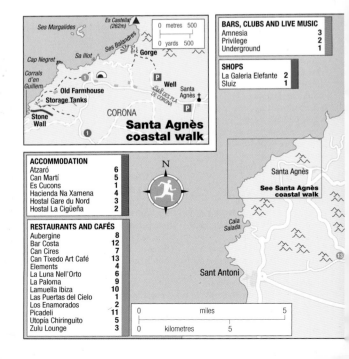

BARS, CLUBS AND LIVE MUSIC

Amnesia	3
Privilege	2
Underground	1

SHOPS

| La Galeria Elefante | 2 |
| Sluiz | 1 |

ACCOMMODATION

Atzaró	6
Can Martí	5
Es Cucons	1
Hacienda Na Xamena	4
Hostal Gare du Nord	3
Hostal La Cigüeña	2

RESTAURANTS AND CAFÉS

Aubergine	8
Bar Costa	12
Can Cires	7
Can Tixedo Art Café	13
Elements	4
La Luna Nell'Orto	6
La Paloma	9
Lamuella Ibiza	10
Las Puertas del Cielo	1
Los Enamorados	2
Picadeli	11
Utopía Chiringuito	5
Zulu Lounge	3

Sant Llorenç

MAP P.58, POCKET MAP D11

Bus #20 from Ibiza Town, May–Oct daily, Nov–April Mon–Sat.

Eight kilometres southwest of Sant Joan, remote **Sant Llorenç** is one of Ibiza's least-visited settlements. The exceptional *La Paloma* restaurant (see page 66) aside, there's not much to the place – a village bar, a handful of houses and the handsome eighteenth-century whitewashed **church**.

Worth a visit is the **Es Amunts Interpretation Centre** (Ctra. Sant Llorenç Mon–Fri 8am–3pm all year). Es Amunts (*amunt* meaning up or above in Catalan) refers to the hilly northern slice of the island, roughly Cala Sant Vincent in the east to Caló des Moro in the west, which has a natural, cultural and geographical identity all of its own. The centre is mainly an educational facility with interesting displays and videos on flora, fauna

and geology, but it also provides details of walks in the area and has guidebooks to borrow free of charge. Outside is a small botanic garden showcasing the area's unique, indigenous species.

Benirràs

MAP P.58

Bus #23 from Ibiza Town, June–Sept daily. Bus #23A from Sant Antoni, June–Sept Sun only. Bus #23P shuttles between the beach and the Sa Plana car park, June–Sept daily. Parking on Sun is restricted in summer and you'll need to use the car park shuttle bus or have a reservation at one of the restaurants.

One of Ibiza's most idyllic beaches, **Benirràs** is a 300m-wide sandy cove set against a backdrop of high, densely forested cliffs. At the mouth of the bay lies **Cap Bernat** – a prominent rock islet that's revered by the spiritually minded. It's said to resemble, variously, a woman at prayer, a giant baby, or the Sphinx.

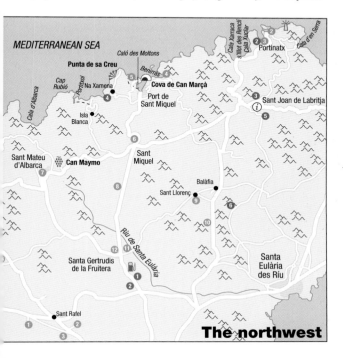

Legendary in hippy folklore, and said to have been the site of wild drug-and-sex orgies in the 1960s, Benirràs's distinctly alternative tendencies persist today, and the beach remains a favourite among Ibiza's New Age community. On Sunday afternoons, groups of drummers gather here to salute the sunset and the beach swarms with dancers and revellers. What once must have been a kind of spiritual pilgrimage is now firmly on the tourist agenda, with coachloads bussed in for the event, which will either enhance or diminish the festival vibe depending on your preferences. Just behind the sands are three unobtrusive beach restaurants, of which *Elements* (see page 66) is undoubtedly the highlight.

Sant Miquel

MAP P.58, POCKET MAP D10
Bus #25 from Ibiza Town, all year Mon–Sat. Bus #22 from Sant Antoni, May–Oct Tues & Thurs. Bus #37 from Santa Eulària, May–Oct Mon & Wed.

Perched high in the glorious Es Amunts hills, **Sant Miquel** is the largest of the villages in this region.

Ball pagès

It's not especially picturesque but it does retain plenty of unhurried, rural character, and you'll find a good mix of locals and visitors in the bars during the summer.

The settlement dates back to the thirteenth century, when the first walls of a fortified church, the **Església de Sant Miquel**, were constructed on the Puig de Missa hilltop, a defensive position some 4km from the sea, giving the original inhabitants a little extra protection from marauding pirates. It's a short, if steep, signposted walk from the village's main street to the small plaça in front of the church, which commands magnificent views over the pine forests and olive groves, and has a small, welcoming bar. *Ball pagès* (folk dancing) displays are staged in the church patio on Thursdays at 6pm (May–Sept) when there's also a craft market (May–Oct 6–10pm).

Port de Sant Miquel

MAP P.58, POCKET MAP C11
Bus #25A from Ibiza Town, May–Oct Mon–Sat. Bus #22 from Sant Antoni, May–Oct Tues & Thurs. Bus #37 from Santa Eulària, May–Oct Mon & Wed.

From Sant Miquel, a scenic road meanders 4km north through a fertile valley to **Port de Sant Miquel**, a spectacular bay that was a tiny fishing harbour and a tobacco smugglers' stronghold until the 1970s. Craggy promontories shelter the inlet's dazzlingly blue, shallow waters, and there's a fine sandy beach, but the bay's beauty is tainted considerably by the presence of two ugly concrete hotel blocks built into the eastern cliffs. Catering almost exclusively to the package tourist trade, Port de Sant Miquel's bars and restaurants are pretty average – the *Port Balansat* is the best for seafood.

Caló des Moltons

MAP P.58
From the western edge of Port de Sant Miquel's beach, a path loops

Cova de Can Marçà

around the shoreline for 200m to a tiny cove, **Caló des Moltons**, where there's a small patch of sand, an excellent *chiringuito* and fine, sheltered swimming. The same trail continues past the beach for another kilometre, climbing through woods to a well-preserved stone defence tower, **Torre des Molar**, from where there are good views of the rugged northern coast towards Portinatx.

Cova de Can Marçà

MAP P.58
Av. Cala Benirràs s/n, Port de Sant Miquel. ☏ 971 334 776, ⓦ covadecanmarsa.com. May–Oct daily 10.30am–7.30pm, Nov–Apr 11am–5.30pm. €11 adults, €7 children.
Just past Port de Sant Miquel's hotel complexes, **Cova de Can Marçà** is a modest-sized cave system that, though unlikely to get speleologists drooling with excitement, is the biggest in Ibiza. The cave, containing impressive stalactites and stalagmites, is about 100,000 years old, and was formed by an underground river that once flowed through the hillside. Entry is by guided tour (in English, Spanish & German)

every half hour in summer and every hour in winter. The pleasant café outside offers great views across the bay to the small island of Illa des Bosc.

Portitxol

MAP P.58
Some 5km northwest of Sant Miquel, the hidden bay of **Portitxol** is one of the most dramatic sights in Ibiza – a fifty-metre-wide, horseshoe-shaped pebbly cove, strewn with giant boulders and a ring of tiny stone-and-brushwood fisherman huts and dwarfed by a monumental backdrop of cliffs that seem to set the bay apart from the rest of the world. In high season, a few adventurous souls work their way to this remote spot for a little secluded snorkelling, but for most of the year Portitxol is largely deserted.

Getting to Portitxol is a bit tricky. From Sant Miquel, the signposted road to Portitxol zigzags up through woods to the Isla Blanca complex of holiday villas. You pass a café-restaurant on the right, after which the road descends, eventually coming to an end at a large dirt car park. Leave your car here and continue downhill on foot. The rocky path twists and turns and, after about 15 minutes, keep your eye out for a high dry stone wall on your left. Where the wall ends, you'll see a narrow path leading off to the left. Take this path instead of continuing on the wider path downhill. Another 20-minute walk along this path through some stunning cliffside scenery and you're at the seashore. For the final descent, the path splits here and there, although by this point the water's edge is in view so it should be clear which way to go. At one point the path forks and the lower path involves edging around the hillside for a short distance using the rope provided. If you'd prefer to avoid this, retrace your steps and take the higher path. It's a 2.5km (30–40min) walk one way; you'll need trainers rather than

Santa Agnès coastal hike

This circular walk (4.5km/2hr from Santa Agnès or 3km/1.5hr from *Las Puertas del Cielo* restaurant) explores some of Ibiza's most remote coastal scenery, along high cliffs and through thick forest, and offers (if you're nimble) the chance of a dip in the sea. From the church in Santa Agnès, follow the paved Camí des Plà de Corona road west past farmhouses and fields of vines, fruit and almond trees. It's a fifteen-minute walk or five-minute drive to *Las Puertas del Cielo*. Just before the restaurant there's a rough dirt track on the right that leads downhill to the sea. Follow the track and the blue arrows that guide you down towards the sea. About 50m before the cliff edge, a small path leads off round the cliff side to the left, indicated by a blue arrow. This path continues southwest around the coastal cliffs, dotted with scrub pine and juniper bushes, keeping about 100m above the sea. The path is narrow and clings precipitously to the cliff side in places – take great care. Where the trail splits, blue arrows indicate the correct path and, after another ten minutes' walking, you pass through the rocky headland of **Cap Negret**. Follow the blue arrows around a wall and continue through overgrown farm terraces before descending to a lovely clearing in the pines, where there's a long-abandoned farmhouse; the small domed stone structure was once a bread oven. Continuing west, you'll pass through a clump of giant reeds, shortly after which you'll reach a fork in the path. Take the right turn downhill through a series of large, overgrown farm terraces, propped up by substantial stone walls. Walk through the terraces past some old water-storage tanks. The route is very close to the sea here, but you'll have to scramble down the rocks for a dip. To return, continue along the inland path up the wooded hillside. The steep route is a little ill-defined at first. When you reach a crumbling stone wall, ignore the paths that lead beyond down to the shore below and instead head uphill to reach a couple of other crumbling walls, where you'll see a much clearer inland path. Follow this path west (right) and continue uphill through a pine-clad valley. After fifteen minutes the trail levels out and descends gently to the Camí des Plà de Corona; turn left, and it's a five-minute walk back to *Las Puertas del Cielo*, or twenty minutes to Santa Agnès.

Sant Mateu d'Albarca

flip flops and to bring your own refreshments.

Sant Mateu d'Albarca

MAP P.58, POCKET MAP C11
Bus #33 from Ibiza Town, all year Mon–Fri.

There's little to the village of **Sant Mateu d'Albarca**, 7km west of Sant Miquel, other than a couple of bars, a whitewashed **church** and the superb restaurant, *Can Cires* (see page 58), which makes the perfect pitstop after a day of exploring the surrounding countryside.

Tourism has barely touched the area, a rustic landscape of small fields of brick-red earth separated by low sandstone walls. Much of the land is given over to **vineyards**, and on the first weekend each December, the village hosts an annual festival in honour of the humble local *vi pagès* (country wine). Less than a kilometre east of the village, the **Can Maymó** vineyard produces 25,000 litres of red and white wine annually and is open for visits year-round (Tues–Sat 11am–2pm & 5–8pm, Sun 10am–1pm).

Cala d'Albarca

MAP P.58

Once the main point of sea access for Sant Mateu, the untouched bay of **Cala d'Albarca**, 4km north of the town, is one of Ibiza's most magnificent. In an island of diminutive cove beaches, its sheer scale is remarkable: a tier of cliffs towers above the three-kilometre-wide bay, and a choppy sea washes the rocky shoreline. There's no beach, and as a result, Cala d'Albarca remains one of Ibiza's best-kept secrets, completely deserted for most of the year.

To get here from Sant Mateu, follow the signs to Cala d'Albarca from the church; after 700m, you reach a junction. Bear left and follow the road through a large vineyard until you another sign guiding you right up a dirt road that leads to the wooded cliffs above Cala d'Albarca. Past the cliffs, the road is in terrible condition, and you'll have to walk the final fifteen minutes down to the beach. When you reach the rugged promontory at the bottom of the dirt road, look out for the natural stone bridge carved out

Plaça de l'Església, Santa Gertrudis de la Fruitera

of the rock by the waves. With the sand-coloured formations of Cap Rubió to the northeast, and brilliant white patches of chalk at the back of the bay, the multi-coloured cliffs are also striking.

Santa Agnès

MAP P.58, POCKET MAP B11
Bus #30 from Ibiza Town, July–Sept Mon–Fri, Oct–June Mon, Wed & Fri. Bus #30 from Sant Antoni, July–Sept Mon–Fri, Oct–June Mon, Wed & Fri.

Some 7km southwest of Sant Mateu, the tiny hamlet of **Santa Agnès** is made up of a scattering of houses, the simple *Sa Palmera* restaurant and the friendly *Can Cosmi* bar. There are no specific sights other than the pretty village church, which dates from 1806. With a patchwork of small, stone-walled fields densely planted with figs, fruit and thousands of almond trees, the countryside here is very beautiful. If you visit in late January or early February, the sea of pink-white almond blossoms is an unforgettable sight.

Santa Gertrudis de la Fruitera

MAP P.58, POCKET MAP C12
Bus #25 from Ibiza Town, all year Mon–Sat. Bus #33 from Ibiza Town, all year Mon–Fri. Bus #22 from Sant Antoni, May–Oct Tues & Thurs. Bus #37 from Santa Eulària, May–Oct Mon & Wed.

Smack in the centre of the island, 11km from Ibiza Town and just off the highway to Sant Miquel, lies **Santa Gertrudis de la Fruitera** ("of the fruits" – the village is known for its crops of apples, apricots, peaches and oranges). It's a small but interesting place with an international – and rather bourgeois – character, and offers a glut of superb bars, restaurants and boutiques out of all proportion to its size. Even in the winter months, tank-like 4WDs and ancient Citröen 2CVs compete for prime parking positions, and a collection of moneyed expats, farmers and locals fills the streetside café terraces below the pretty eighteenth century **Església de Santa Gertrudis**.

Shops

La Galeria Elefante

MAP P.58

Ctra. Sant Miguel, km 3.2, Santa Gertrudis.
☎ 971 197 017, Ⓦ lagaleriaelefante.com.
Mon–Sat 10am–8pm.

Beautiful, ethnically-inspired clothes, accessories and homeware sourced from around the world and lovingly curated by Victoria Elefante, who also runs the yoga and wellness studio next door.

Sluiz

MAP P.58

Ctra. Sant Miquel km 4, Santa Gertrudis.
☎ 971 931 206, Ⓦ sluiz.com. Daily 10am–10pm.

6000 square metres packed with colourful and eccentric home decor, clothes and object d'arts you never knew you wanted. More of a shopping experience than a shopping centre, it's a fun place to browse and host to various Sunday events in winter. See website for details.

Restaurants and cafés

Aubergine

MAP P.58

Ctra. Sant Miquel km 9.9, 1km before Sant Miquel. ☎ 971 090 055, Ⓦ aubergineibiza.com. March to mid-Oct daily 9.30am–midnight, mid-Oct to mid-Jan Wed–Sun 9.30am–6pm, mid-Jan to Feb closed.

"From farm to table" is the motto of this pretty restaurant serving up imaginative dishes using ingredients from the surrounding organic vegetable garden, such as beetroot and quinoa burger with goat's cheese (€17) or stuffed aubergine with beef and lamb (€19). In summer, there's live electro-acoustic music on Tues, Thurs and Sun evenings, plus an artisanal night market on Sundays.

Bar Costa

MAP P.58

Santa Gertrudis. Daily 8am–1am.

Richly atmospheric village bar, with a cavernous interior and narrow, sociable pavement terrace. Legs of *jamón serrano* garnish the ceiling, while the walls are covered in paintings – most donated by artists to clear their bar bills. Has a decent menu and the most famous *tostadas* in Ibiza.

Can Cires

MAP P.58

Camí de S Plà s/n, Sant Mateu. ☎ 971 805 551, Ⓦ cancires.com. Open all year except Nov, Mon & Wed–Sun noon–midnight.

Highly recommended restaurant serving traditional Ibizan dishes with touches from Alsace, reflecting the origins of its owners. Highlights include the chateaubriand (€28), steak tartar (€28), squid with sobrassada (€18) and the tarte flambée. Popular with locals, it also caters well to the hard-earned appetites of walkers exploring the beautiful area around Sant Mateu.

Bar Costa

Elements

MAP P.58

Cala Benirràs. ☎ 971 333 136, ⓦ elements-ibiza.com. May–Sept daily 11am–11pm, Oct–April daily 11am–10pm.

Spacious and stylish restaurant, bar, shop and massage area all rolled into one on the beach at Benirràs. The extensive menu reflects the chef's Italian roots, with homemade pasta the speciality. Try the grilled tuna 'tagliata' with cherry tomatoes and anchovy foam (€30) or the tagliatelle with seafood (€21). Sunday is drumming day at Benirràs and the restaurant becomes more of a beach club, with DJs providing the sounds while performance artists and projectors provide the visuals.

La Luna Nell'Orto

MAP P.58

C/ des Port s/n, Sant Miquel. ☎ 971 334 599, ⓦ lalunanellorto.com. April, May & Oct Mon & Wed–Sun, June–Sept daily, 8pm–midnight.

Exceptional Italian food served in a romantic garden attached to

La Luna Nell'Orto

a traditional, rustic farmhouse, complete with candles, flowers, fig trees and occasional live music. Famous for its homemade pasta, such as the squid ink tagliatelle with seafood (€25), and other Mediterranean dishes, such as octopus with wakame seaweed chimichurri (€26).

La Paloma

MAP P.58

C/ Can Pou 4, Sant Llorenç. ☎ 971 325 543, ⓦ palomaibiza.com. Daily 12.30–4.30pm & 7.30–11.30pm.

Extremely pretty and popular garden restaurant serving a wide range of Mediterranean and Israeli dishes during the day (minced lamb stuffed focaccia €14, homemade pizza €8, salads around €13) and a more expensive Italian menu at night. The wine list is 100% organic and much of the produce is sourced from the surrounding garden. Cash only during the day; booking essential.

Las Puertas del Cielo

MAP P.58

Camí des Plà de Corona km 2, Santa Agnès. ☎ 680 964 796. Mid-June to mid-Sept Tues–Sun 1–5pm & 8–10pm, mid-Sept to mid-June Tues–Sun 12.30pm–5.30pm.

Small café-restaurant in a secluded location on the clifftop above Santa Agnès overlooking the islet of Ses Margalides. The views and sunsets are so wonderful here, it's easy to understand how the area gained its name, Heaven's Gate (*puertas del cielo*). Serves traditional Ibizan food (mixed paella, min 2pp, €17.50) and homemade desserts (*flaó* and *greixonera*, €4.50).

Los Enamorados

MAP P.58

C/ de Portinatx 103, Portinatx. ☎ 971 337 549, ⓦ losenamoradosibiza.com.

Built on top of fishermen's huts overlooking the pretty bay of Es Portixol, this Asian-fusion restaurant is Portinatx's best.

Seating is on a high-ceilinged terrace at rustic tables and the food is delicious. Try the crunchy fresh prawn won ton with chili sauce (€16) or avocado gazpacho (€14) followed by the slow cooked octopus skewers (€19).

Lamuella Ibiza

MAP P.58

Ctra. Sant Joan km 13, Sant Llorenç. ☎ 971 325 356, Ⓦ lamuella-ibiza.com. May–Oct daily 9am–midnight.

All Ibiza concept restaurant elements are here: elegant setting, beautiful staff, locally sourced ingredients, plus DJs, yoga and a large play area for kids. The Med/Middle eastern fusion menu is superb and designed to share on large plates. Favourites include the BBQ crispy duck (€17) and the langoustine Vietnamese pancakes (€16). The tasting menu, while not cheap (€85 excluding drinks, reserve 24hr in advance) is well worth the splurge.

Picadeli

MAP P.58

Ctra. PM-804, 9, Santa Gertrudis. ☎ 971 197 121, Ⓦ picadeli-ibiza.com. Mon–Fri 8.30am–8pm, Sat 10am–8pm.

High quality, homemade organic food to takeaway: €12.50 for three choices (one protein, one cereal and one veg). Popular dishes include the Mexican salad with avocado and the soba noodles with cashew nuts and mango. Also sells homemade cakes, a wide range of organic wines and juices and tubs of hummus and baba ghanoush (€4.50).

Utopía Chiringuito

MAP P.58

Caló des Moltons, Port de Sant Miquel. ☎ 642 734 094. June–Sept daily 9.30am–11.30pm, May & Oct daily 9.30am–9.30pm. Cash only.

Ibiza's prettiest *chiringuito* in an idyllic setting at Caló des Moltons.

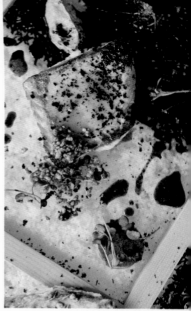

Lamuella Ibiza

Barbecued fish is the speciality, cooked on the beach in front of you, with a choice of king prawns (€20), squid, sardines (€15.50), or a mix to share, all served with a generous portion of veg and potatoes. On Friday nights, they host Sardinada: as many barbecued sardines as you can eat for €15. Reservations only possible for 6 or more.

Zulu Lounge

MAP P.58

s'Arenal Petite, Portinatx. June–Sept daily 9am–3am, May & Oct 9am–1am.

Your best bet in provincial Portinatx for a stylish bar, this place's alcove tables are set under the rockface that forms the rear of the bay. There's an extensive cocktail list, a menu of Mexican and Mediterranean dishes, and chillout sounds. The bar's excellent location makes for a perfect sundowner.

Sant Antoni and around

The tourist resort of Sant Antoni (San Antonio) is as bombastic as you'll find in Europe. High-rise, concrete-clad and blatantly brash, San An (as it's known) primarily draws crowds of young Brits bent on a relentless pursuit of unbridled hedonism. Things can get pretty messy in the West End, but there are plenty of less frenetic activities on offer. On the west side of town an array of stylish bars line the promenade, which connects the Sunset Strip with Caló des Moro and just beyond are the pretty bays of Cala Gració and Gracioneta. Sant Antoni's harbour, a sickle-shaped expanse of sapphire water that laps s'Arenal beach, offers a staggering array of water sports, while a short bus or boat ride away, you'll find some of Ibiza's most impressive cove beaches and swimming spots.

The harbourfront

MAP P.72, POCKET MAP G7–G9

Sant Antoni's main **harbourfront** begins at the **Egg**, a white sculpture erected to honour a tenuous claim that Christopher Columbus was born on the island. Inside the hollow structure is a miniature wooden caravel, modelled on the fifteenth-century vessels in which the explorer sailed. West of the Egg, the broad promenade has a luxuriant collection of tropical palms, rubber plants and flowering shrubs, and a series of flashy modern fountains, dramatically illuminated at night. The harbourfront is lined with stalls selling pretty much every water-based activity you can think of: from parasailing, SUP boarding, fly-boarding and jet skiing to seabobs, sunset cruises, snorkelling tours and fishing trips. Water taxis also offer a service around the bay to nearby hotels while regular ferries run to Port des Torrent and Calas Gració, Salada, Bassa and Comte.

The promenade narrows once you've passed a statue of a fisherman, complete with nets and catch; opposite here is the **Moll Vell**, the old dock, where you'll often see fishermen mending their nets and fixing reed lobster-pots.

Arrival and information

Buses all depart from the bus station on the east side of town off Av. de Portmany. Bus #3 serves Ibiza Town (all year daily) plus nightbus #3 (June–Sept daily); bus #8 also runs to Ibiza Town via Sant Josep (July & Aug daily, Sept–June Mon–Sat). Bus #9 (mid-May to mid-Oct daily) connects San An with the airport. Boats (all May–Oct only) depart from the harbourfront on Passeig de ses Fonts. Sant Antoni's **tourist information office** (May–Oct Mon–Fri 10am–8pm, Sat & Sun 10am–2pm & 5–8pm; Nov–April daily 10am–2pm) is on the harbourfront, just west of the Egg.

The San An scene

San An's importance as a breeding ground for **dance music** talent is undeniable. All the main players who kickstarted the UK's acid house revolution in 1987 holidayed in the town at a time when the bars and clubs in virtually every other European resort were still playing party chart hits. By the mid-1990s, as clubbing became much more of a mainstream phenomenon, Ibiza's clubbing kudos and reputation for musical authenticity drew young British holidaymakers en masse to party in San An and experience the island's **unique scene**.

But by 2003 the music had become pretty lifeless, with an army of wannabe DJs playing near-identical house mixes and the innovation unleashed by acid house conspicuous by its absence. Enter Manumission, who, in typically provocative manner, declared "guitars are the new turntables", before announcing a summer season called Ibiza Rocks, featuring the cream of emerging indie talent from the UK. Against the odds, Ibiza Rocks was a triumph and for the next decade, the brand reigned in San An, pulling off gigs featuring the likes of the Kaiser Chiefs, Soulwax and the Prodigy, and acquiring their own hotel-venue in 2008 (*Ibiza Rocks Hotel*, see page 117).

In recent years, trends have changed again as stricter licensing laws have been introduced alongside an emerging preference among younger visitors for daytime, outdoor parties – much to the annoyance of the original clubs, some of whom had invested large sums of money adding roofs to outdoor spaces. In 2017, even Ibiza Rocks changed tack to focus on DJs and pool parties rather than rock gigs, with names such as Craig David, Elrow and Stormzy now headlining the show.

Further west, you pass the marina and modern Club Nàutic (Yacht Club) building before you reach a 400m-long dock that juts into the harbour, from where huge ferries head for mainland Spain. Just north of the harbourfront up C/ Ample is the large **Església de Sant Antoni**, a handsome, whitewashed structure with a twin belfry and a pleasantly shady side-porch. The building mainly dates from the late seventeenth century, though there has been a chapel here since 1305.

The West End
MAP P.72, POCKET MAP G7

The island's most raucous bar zone, the notorious **West End** – described by writer Paul Richardson as "The Blackpool of Ibiza, cheerfully vulgar,

The West End

The Sunset Strip

There's nothing subtle about this almost entirely British enclave of wall-to-wall disco-bars and pubs, interspersed with the odd hole-in-the-wall kebab joint or Chinese restaurant serving fry-up breakfasts. In summer the streets are overrun with sunburnt teenagers in football shirts; understandably, few Ibizans would dream of drinking around here and you'll be able to tell straight away if it's the kind of place you'll love or hate. In general drinks are much cheaper than Sunset Strip or Ibiza Town averages, and as the disco-bars are usually free, it's an inexpensive place to strut your stuff.

The Sunset Strip

MAP P.72, POCKET MAP E7

Stretching for 250m along the rocky shoreline between C/ General Balanzat and C/ Vara de Rey, Sant Antoni's legendary **Sunset Strip** of chillout bars is the

unashamedly unglamorous" – spreads over a network of streets centred around C/ Santa Agnès.

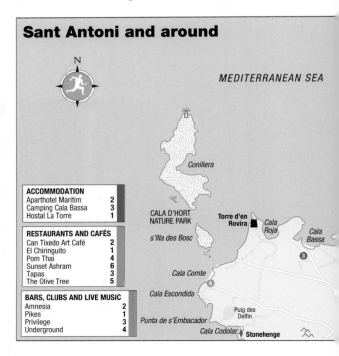

Sant Antoni and around

N

MEDITERRANEAN SEA

Conillera

CALA D'HORT NATURE PARK

s'Illa des Bosc

Torre d'en Rovira

Cala Roja

Cala Bassa

Cala Comte

Cala Escondida

Cala Codolar

Punta de s'Embacador

Puig des Delfín

Stonehenge

ACCOMMODATION

Aparthotel Maritim	2
Camping Cala Bassa	3
Hostal La Torre	1

RESTAURANTS AND CAFÉS

Can Tixedo Art Café	2
El Chiringuito	1
Pom Thai	4
Sunset Ashram	6
Tapas	3
The Olive Tree	5

BARS, CLUBS AND LIVE MUSIC

Amnesia	2
Pikes	1
Privilege	3
Underground	4

resort at its most sophisticated. A graceful promenade extends across the coastal rocks, and the bars have attractive terraces. The location can be captivating around sunset, when all eyes turn west to watch the sun sinking into the blood-red sea, to a background of ambient soundscapes.

Until 1993, there was only one chillout bar, the ground-breaking *Café del Mar*, along this entire stretch of coast, and it was very much the preserve of in-the-know clubbers and islanders. But since then the scene has proliferated and there now dozens of such bars, *Café Mambo* being perhaps the most famous (see page 80), plus large crowds, with the sunset spectacle very much part of most people's "Ibiza experience".

Caló des Moro
MAP P.72, POCKET MAP E6

North of the Sunset Strip, the promenade continues for some 500m to **Caló des Moro**, a tiny cove with a small patch of sand surrounded by a scattering of hotel and apartment blocks. The opening of several swanky bar-restaurants here has helped Caló des Moro become San An's most happening location in recent years, rivalling the Sunset Strip as *the* premier chillout zone. The bay makes an inviting place for a dip, with shallow, turquoise water.

s'Arenal
MAP P.72, POCKET MAP G8

South of the Egg, slimline s'Arenal beach hugs the shore as far as the Punta des Molí promontory. Though not the best beach in the area, it's the nearest one to town and the sands get very busy in summer. A section of the sea is partitioned off from jet-skiers and boats so that swimmers can enjoy themselves safely, while bordering

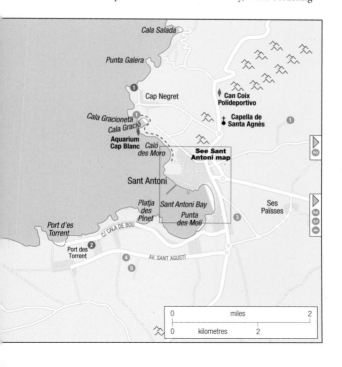

SANT ANTONI AND AROUND

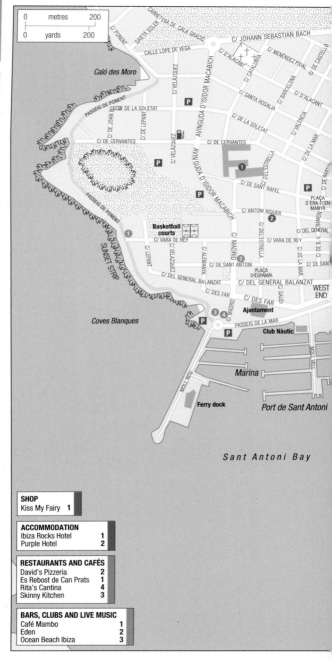

SHOP
Kiss My Fairy   **1**

ACCOMMODATION
Ibiza Rocks Hotel   **1**
Purple Hotel   **2**

RESTAURANTS AND CAFÉS
David's Pizzeria   **2**
Es Rebost de Can Prats   **1**
Rita's Cantina   **4**
Skinny Kitchen   **3**

BARS, CLUBS AND LIVE MUSIC
Café Mambo   **1**
Eden   **2**
Ocean Beach Ibiza   **3**

Sant Antoni

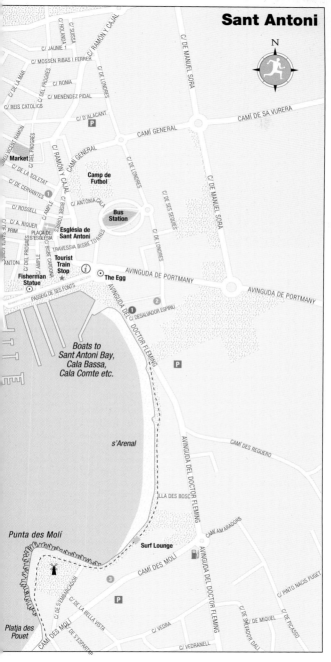

N

C/ SUISSA
C/ ROLANDA
C/ JAUME 1
C/ MOSSÈN RIBAS I FERRER
C/ DE LA MAR
C/ ROMA
C/ DEL PROGRÈS
C/ MENÉNDEZ PIDAL
C/ REIS CATOLICS
C/ RAMÓN Y CAJAL
C/ DE LONDRES
C/ DE MANUEL SORÀ
CAMÍ DE SA VURERA
C/ D'ALACANT
CAMÍ GENERAL
C/ MENÉNCANT RAMON
C/ DEL PROGRÈS
Market
C/ DE LA SOLETAT
C/ DE CERVANTES
CAMÍ GENERAL
C/ RAMÓN Y CAJAL
Camp de Futbol
C/ DE LONDRES
C/ ROSSELL
C/ AMPLE
C/ ANTÒNIA CALA
C/ BISBE TORRES
Bus Station
C/ DE SES SEQUIES
C/ DE MANUEL SORÀ
C/ A. RIQUER
PLAÇA DE S'ESGLÉSIA
Església de Sant Antoni
C/ DE SANT VICENT PRIM
ANTONI
C/ DEL PROGRÈS
C/ AMPLE
C/ BISBE CARDONA
TRAVESSIA BISBE TORRES
C/ DE LONDRES
Tourist Train Stop
The Egg
AVINGUDA DE PORTMANY
Fisherman Statue
PASSEIG DE SES FONTS
AVINGUDA DEL
C/ DESALVADOR ESPIRIU
AVINGUDA DE PORTMANY
Boats to Sant Antoni Bay, Cala Bassa, Cala Comte etc.
DOCTOR FLEMING
P
s'Arenal
AVINGUDA DEL DOCTOR FLEMING
CAMÍ DES REGUERO
ILLA DES BOSC
Punta des Molí
Surf Lounge
CAMÍ AMARADORS
CAMÍ DES MOLÍ
AVINGUDA DEL DOCTOR FLEMING
C/ PINTO NACIS PUGET
P
C/ DE S'EMBARCADOR
C/ DE LA BELLA VISTA
C/ DES MOLÍ
C/ DE S'ESPARTAR
C/ VEDRA
C/ VEDRANELL
C/ DE SALVADOR DALÍ
C/ DE MIQUEL
C/ DE PICASSO
Platja des Pouet

Aquarium Cap Blanc

the beach are some stylish bar-cafés. A landscaped, palm-lined harbourside promenade runs along the back of the bay.

Jutting into the harbourfront at the southern end of the promenade, past a row of block-like hotel complexes, an imposing, old white windmill with warped wooden sails crowns the Punta des Molí promontory, a quiet, landscaped spot planted with olive trees, lavender and rosemary bushes.

Aquarium Cap Blanc

MAP P.70
Bus #1 (Cala Gració stop) from Sant Antoni, April–Oct daily. Ctra. Cala Gració s/n, Sant Antoni. ☎ 663 945 475, ⓦ aquariumcapblanc.com. June–Sept daily 10am–10pm, April, May & Oct 10am–9.30pm. Adults €5, children €3.
Further along the coast from Caló des Moro, set in an old smugglers' cave on the south side of Cala Gració, is the modest **Aquarium Cap Blanc**. The centre is home to a collection of sluggish-looking Mediterranean sealife, including lobster, moray eel, wrasse and octopus. It's well organized and popular with children, with wooden walkways above pools containing the sea creatures. Entrance to the Aquarium is via a small bar perched on the cliff-edge at the end of a narrow coastal path overlooking the bay – a destination in its own right, especially for sunset.

Cala Gració

MAP P.70, POCKET MAP B12
Bus #1 from Sant Antoni, April–Oct daily.
A kilometre northwest of Caló des Moro, around the rocky fringes of Sant Antoni Bay, is the small but gorgeous beach of **Cala Gració**, an elongated patch of fine white sand which stretches back 100m from the sea. The shallow water is wonderfully calm and clear, and only gets really busy at the height of summer. A simple café-restaurant, *Restaurante Bresca* (May–Oct daily 10am–8pm), offers the usual seafood and rice dishes as well as drinks and cocktails.

Cala Gracioneta

MAP P.70
Bus #1 (Cala Gració stop) from Sant Antoni,

April–Oct daily.

From the fishing huts on the north side of Cala Gració, a path clings to the shoreline, leading after 100m to a second hidden bay, the exceptionally beautiful and peaceful Cala Gracioneta. This little gem of a beach is barely 30m wide, but has exquisite pale sand, backed by pines; the shallow, sheltered waters here heat up to almost bathtub temperatures by late summer. The bay also boasts a decent restaurant, *Chiringuito* (see page 78), where food is served practically on the sand.

Punta Galera

MAP P.70, POCKET MAP D14

Bus #1 (Stella Maris stop) from Sant Antoni, April–Oct daily.

North from Cala Gracioneta, the isolated bay of **Punta Galera** is popular with naturists and hippies. Bizarre eroded cliffs of stratified stone and a series of shelf-like rock terraces (many painted with New Age doodles) form natural shelves for sunbathing, and the sapphire waters offer excellent snorkelling. In summer, it's common for entrepreneurial hippy types to set up shop selling mojitos and other fruit cocktails (usually around €10) from an ice box.

To get to Punta Galera by road, take the Cala Salada turn-off from the Sant Antoni–Santa Agnès highway, continue downhill until you reach a white arched gateway across the road, where the road splits, then bear left downhill towards the sea.

Cala Salada

MAP P.70, POCKET MAP B11

Bus #34 from Sant Antoni, end May–Sept daily.

Ringed by a protective barrier of steep, pine-clad hills, the turquoise waters of **Cala Salada** are some of the most inviting in Ibiza. Apart from a line of stick-and-thatch fishermen's huts, a solitary villa and a simple seafood restaurant

(May–Oct daily; Nov–April Sat & Sun), popular with locals, there's nothing here but the sea and beach. It is, however, one of the best places in the Pitiuses to watch the sunset, ideally in winter, when the sun sinks into the ocean between the gateway-like outlines of the islands of Conillera and Bosc. Unsurprisingly, its beauty is hardly a secret and with only two short stretches of sand, it can get very crowded throughout the summer months. Parking restrictions were recently introduced to control numbers and in high season you may be required to leave your car at the Can Coix car park and take the shuttle bus (€2).

To the north of Cala Salada, about two hundred metres across the bay, is an even more peaceful sandy cove, **Cala Saldeta** – you can either swim over or follow a path that winds around the fishing huts.

Sant Antoni Bay

MAP P.70, POCKET MAP B12

Bus #2 (all year) and #6 (May–Oct) from Sant Antoni, daily. Boats from Sant Antoni, May–Oct daily.

San Antoni Bay

From the Punta des Molí promontory, C/ Cala de Bou heads west around the bay, between apartment and hotel blocks and the attendant commercial sprawl. Plenty of British visitors booked on last-minute deals end up in hotels around here, and though this strip is unremittingly touristy, it tends to attract more families than San An itself, and the atmosphere is correspondingly less boisterous.

The best beach on this stretch is **Platja des Pinet** (or Platja d'en Xinxó). It's certainly nothing special – a small sandy cove, barely 100m wide – but offers safe swimming in sheltered waters and a few cheap shoreside snack bars.

Port d'es Torrent

MAP P.70, POCKET MAP B12
Bus #2 (all year) and #6 (May–Oct) from Sant Antoni, daily. Boats from Sant Antoni, May–Oct daily.

The coastal road around Sant Antoni Bay comes to a halt at the pretty, sandy cove of **Port d'es**

Torrent, named after a seasonal stream which originates on Ibiza's highest peak, Sa Talaia (see page 83), and empties into the small bay. Nestled at the end of a deep inlet, Port d'es Torrent's sands are packed with families lounging on sunbeds and splashing about in the calm water during the summer; for the rest of the year, it's empty save for the odd fisherman.

Of the three restaurants here, *Deeva Beach Site* has the best beach-side location (W deevabeachsite. com) and provides live music, DJs and occasional fireworks in the evening.

Cala Bassa

MAP P.70, POCKET MAP B12
Buses #7 from Sant Antoni, June to mid-Sept daily. Boats from Sant Antoni, May–Oct daily.

Cala Bassa is one of the most popular beaches in the Sant Antoni area: a fine, 250-metre-wide sandy beach set in a striking horseshoe-shaped bay, ringed by low cliffs and

Cala Bassa

sabina pines. There are plenty of sunbeds and umbrellas to rent and three large café-restaurants, as well as a wonderful view of the hump-shaped coastal outcrop of Cap Nunó and the wooded hills of the island's northwest. The sparkling waters have been awarded Blue Flag status and there are plenty of watersports on offer, as well as a roped-off area for swimmers. Cala Bassa tends to get very busy in high season, but peace returns and the beach clears by 7pm, when the last buses and boats depart.

Cala Comte

MAP P.70, POCKET MAP A12
Bus #4 from Sant Antoni, June to mid-Sept daily. Boats from Sant Antoni, May–Oct daily.

Though there are only two small patches of golden sand, it's easy to see why people rave about **Cala Comte** – and fill it with beach towels and hubbub during high summer – with its gin-clear water, superb ocean vistas and spectacular sunsets. There's also the added attraction of *Sunset Ashram* café-restaurant (see page 79) behind the sands, offering healthy food and a relaxed vibe.

Just to the south is the inlet of Cala Escondida, where there are two more tiny sandy bays – nicer and quieter than Cala Comte and popular with naturists – plus an excellent *chiringuito*.

Cala Codolar

MAP P.70, POCKET MAP A12
Bus #4 from Sant Antoni, June to mid-Sept daily.

About 2km south of Cala Comte, diminutive **Cala Codolar** is very pretty indeed, with pale sand and clear waters sheltered by the rocky headland to the north, though it can get crowded in high season with tourists from the *Club Delfín* hotel just above the bay. There's a good *chiringuito* serving burgers and salads from €46, with a few tables on the beach and sunbeds to

Sunbathers at Cala Comte

rent (June–Oct daily 11am–8pm). Fun Kayaks Ibiza (☎691 655 614, ⓦfunkayaksibiza.com) run magical kayak tours from here, as well as from other nearby *calas*.

Stonehenge

MAP P.70
Bus #4 from Sant Antoni, June to mid-Sept daily.

From the back of Cala Codolar, a well-trodden path leads over the headland to the south and it's about a 5–10min walk to a rocky plateau where 13 extraordinary monoliths stand proud. The structure's real name is Time and Space and was created by artist Andrew Rogers for Guy Laliberté (founder of Cirque de Soleil), who allegedly received a huge fine for building it without permission. This being Ibiza, rumours of its strong magnetic vibrations or it being a landing beacon for UFOs abound. To the left of the monoliths, away from sea, you'll find the 'magic doors', two engraved wooden doors perfectly positioned so that one frames the other and then Es Vedrà beyond.

Shop

Kiss My Fairy

MAP P.72, POCKET MAP G8
Av. Doctor Fleming 9, Sant Antoni. ☎ 971
803 561, ⓦ kissmyfairy.com

Specialist fancy dress and beauty salon with a team of hair-stylists, make-up artists and body painters eager to transform the San An hordes into glittery birds of paradise, sultry wild cats or anything else they fancy. Body painting prices range from €8 for eye glitter up to €50 for half torso, while a cut and blow dry for women is €35.

Restaurants and cafés

Can Tixedo Art Café

MAP P.58
Ctra. Sant Rafel a Santa Agnès km 5.
ⓦ cantixedo.com, ☎ 971 345 248. July
& Aug daily 8am–2am, April–June &
Sept–Oct daily 8am–midnight, Nov–March
Tues–Sun 8am–midnight.

Kiss My Fairy

Located at the crossroads opposite Forada market (Sat 10am–4pm) out in the countryside of Buscastell, this wonderful, buzzy rural café-restaurant serves pre-prepared tapas all day from a long and varied menu. Portions are small and designed to share with lots of options for veggies, such as the excellent spinach lasagne (€7) or lentil salad (€4.80). The art exhibitions on display inside change every two weeks and there are occasional DJs and live performances in the evening.

David's Pizzeria

MAP P.72, POCKET MAP F7
C/ Madrid 12, Sant Antoni. ⓦ davidsibiza.
com, ☎ 971 340 470. Mon–Sat
noon–12.30am.

Offers a wide range of Italian and French dishes but its high quality pizzas are what most people come for. The menu includes all the classics, lots of options for veggies plus several specialty pizzas; try the Forestiere with mushrooms, goat's cheese, cream and olives for €11. The fixed day-time 3-course menu plus drink is good value at €13.50 – available until 8.30pm.

Chiringuito

MAP P.70
Cala Gracioneta ☎ 971 348 338. May–Oct
daily 10.30am–5.30pm & 7–11pm.

Enjoys a sublime setting right by the water's edge in a sandy cove – it's especially pretty at night, when the restaurant owners float candles in the bay's sheltered waters. The straightforward, moderately priced menu includes fish, paella and delicious barbecued meats, and there's a decent wine list.

Es Rebost de Can Prats

MAP P.72, POCKET MAP G7
C/ Cervantes 4, Sant Antoni.
ⓦ esrebostdecanprats.com, ☎ 971 346
252. Mon & Wed–Sun 1–4pm & 8pm–
midnight. Closed Jan.

Just a few blocks north of Ibiza's brashest tourist zone is one of its most traditional restaurants. Set in a 100-year-old converted town-house, Es Rebost de Can Prats (meaning 'the Prats family pantry') serves traditional cuisine in a series of small rooms whose walls are covered in Ibizan art, craft and memorabilia. This is the place to try local specialties, such as *Sofrit Pagès* (meat and potato stew, €16) or slow-cooked shoulder of lamb (€16.50).

Pom Thai

MAP P.70

Av. Sant Agustí 73–75, Cala de Bou. Ⓦ facebook.com/pomthairestaurant/, ☏ 971 078 182. March–Dec daily 7pm–midnight.

Highly recommended Thai restaurant set in the lovely patio garden of an old traditional house on Av. Sant Agustí. The outdoor seating centres around a small, tranquil pool with palms and Thai parasols providing shade in the afternoon and lanterns and candles the mood lighting in the evening. There's a great range of starters and dishes can be prepared as spicy as you like; the Penang curry (chicken, beef, prawn or veg, €12–18) is a firm favourite. Also does takeaways.

Rita's Cantina

MAP P.72, POCKET MAP F8

Paseo Marítimo, Sant Antoni. ☏ 971 343 387, Ⓦ ritascantina.com. Daily 8am–1am. Stylish, high-ceilinged and atmospheric bar-restaurant that stands apart from some of its white-plastic neighbours on the Sant Antoni strip. Dutch-run and popular with locals and holiday-makers alike, Rita's is famous for its breakfasts and Indonesian food, such as the Nasi Goreng (€8.50). It's open year-round.

Skinny Kitchen

MAP P.72, POCKET MAP F8

Passeig de la Mar 20, Sant Antoni. Ⓦ skinnykitchen.co, ☏ 603 698 241. March–Nov daily 9am–11pm.

Skinny Kitchen

With its healthy bites, wraps and protein bowls, this attractive diner is a welcome addition to the San An promenade. The décor is smart and urban, complete with London-pub retro tiles, while the food is tasty, hearty and filling; mains include the coconut cod curry (€14.95) and the salmon and quinoa salad bowl (€14.95). Dishes are tagged as gluten-free, veggie or vegan, or invite you to 'muscle up' and 'get lean'.

Sunset Ashram

MAP P.70

Cala Comte ☏ 661 347 222, Ⓦ sunsetashram.com. March–Oct daily 10am–midnight.

Looking out over the beach, this is a beautiful place to relax and dine as the sun sinks into the Med. International dishes include a range of salads, curries (such as tofu or prawn yellow curry, €25), pad thai (€23) and steaks or fresh fish, including red tuna tataki (€32). There's also a beach-clothing and accessory store, a cocktail bar (cocktails from €10) and nightly DJ sets – see website for details.

Café Mambo

Tapas

MAP P.70

Camino des Reguero 4, Sant Antoni. ☎ 971 341 125, ⓦ tapasrestaurantibiza.com. April–end Oct, daily 4pm–midnight.

Tapas restaurant and lounge bar is a bit of a walk from central Sant Antoni but their creative adaptations of standard tapas are above average and worth the trip. Try the Popeye (cooked spinach with cream, parmesan and minced beef, €6.50) or the jackfruit and pumpkin noodles in Hoisin sauce (€6.75). Good range of veggie options available.

The Olive Tree

MAP P.70

C/ Cantabria 40, Cala de Bou. ☎ 971 340 907. Daily except Mon 5pm–midnight, Sun (winter only) 1–7pm.

Top notch UK-style gastro pub serving classics such as slow roast pork belly with mash potato, greens and sage jus (€14). The menu changes daily to suit whatever's best and freshest at the market that day. The Sunday lunches (winter only) are legendary among island residents.

Bars, clubs and live music

Amnesia

MAP P.58

Ctra. Sant Antoni km 5, Sant Rafel. ☎ 934 082 018, ⓦ amnesia.es. June–Oct. Entrance €40–60.

A lowly farmhouse forty years ago, *Amnesia* became a hangout for hippies in the 1970s, an after-hours club in the 1980s and then the most fashionable club on the island with an underground musical policy that encompassed dark minimal proto-house tunes and electro club hits. This spirit of innovation has endured and the club has worked with key promoters including Cream, Sven Vath's Cocoon and Elrow, while maintaining their own *espuma* (foam) parties. The vast warehouse-like main room is the place to rave and its huge dancefloor – studded with speaker towers – is ideally suited to progressive house, trance and techno.

Café Mambo

MAP P.72, POCKET MAP E7

C/ Vara de Rey 40, Sant Antoni. ☎ 971 346 638, ⓦ cafemamboibiza.com. May–Oct daily 10am–4am.

A classic haunt on the Sunset Strip with a deserved reputation for ambient tunes and strong cocktails (€10 before 5pm, about €15 after). Famed for its big-name DJs, party nights and amazing sunsets.

Eden

MAP P.72, POCKET MAP H7

C/ Salvador Espiriu s/n, Sant Antoni. ⓦ edenibiza.com. June–Sept. Entrance €25–40.

Eden gives its loyal and mainly British crowd exactly what they want – a raver's delight of pounding house and techno, plenty of club anthems and an orgiastic party atmosphere. The club's unpretentiousness means it's never going to be the most fashionable place, but it can claim to be one of the top dogs in San An and to have one of the most impressive sound systems on the island.

Ocean Beach Ibiza

MAP P.72, POCKET MAP G9
C/ des Molí 12–14, Sant Antoni Bay. ☎ 971 803 260, ⓦ oceanbeachibiza.com. July & Aug noon–midnight, May, June & Sept noon–10pm. General admission €10–30 depending on event.

Hugely popular with the bikini- and glitter-clad fashionistas of Sant Antoni, Ocean Beach ticks all the beach club boxes: 6000-square-metre swimming pool, sunset roof terrace, VIP area, day beds for hire with champagne drinks packages, plus large crowds of young, fun twenty-somethings up for a good time. Gets very busy, particularly on Fridays when resident DJs play a mix of club classics and current tunes at the popular pool party.

Pikes

MAP P.70
Camí Sa Vorera, 3km east of Sant Antoni ☎ 971 342 222, ⓦ pikesibiza.com. May–Oct.

Legendary hotel/party venue run by the Ibiza Rocks crew famous for its (in)famous guests (George Michael, Grace Jones, Freddie Mercury, among others), the poolside bar (of Club Tropicana fame), an eclectic array of artwork and super fun party nights. DJ Harvey has a residency here and the popular funk, soul and disco outfit Melon Bomb put on regular nights throughout the summer. Parties are free, but you'll need to put your name on the guest list to get in, see website for details.

Privilege

MAP P.58
Urbanización Sant Rafel s/n, Sant Rafel. ☎ 971 198 160, ⓦ privilegeibiza.com. May–Oct. Entrance €35–50.

Listed in *The Guinness Book of Records* as the world's largest club, *Privilege* is also home to the biggest club nights on the planet, with a capacity of up to 10,000 punters. As you enter, the sheer scale of the place becomes apparent, with a huge main dancefloor before you, a large stage at the back plus a DJ plinth suspended above the swimming pool. The club also boasts fourteen bars, a VIP zone on the upper level as well as the famous glass-encased Vista club with views over towards Ibiza Town, the perfect place to be at sunrise.

Underground

MAP P.58
Ctra. Sant Antoni km 7. ☎ 971 198 015, ⓦ ibizaunderground.com. April–Oct.

One of Ibiza's least-hyped club-bars, set in a converted farmhouse just north of the main cross-island highway. With a reputation for being about the music rather than the money, and for booking more unusual, up-and-coming artists, the events here tend to attract an older bunch of in-the-know islanders and well-connected international faces. The dancefloor has a potent sound system but the vibe is intimate and there are adjacent lounge-around rooms and a beautiful garden terrace.

Privilege

The south

Southern Ibiza is wildly beautiful and physically diverse, encompassing the island's highest peak, Sa Talaia, the shimmering Salines saltpans and drowsy one-horse villages, as well as a craggy coast staked with defence towers. The coastline is lapped by warm, transparent waters and endowed with more than a dozen gorgeous beaches. The region has only three resorts – the quiet bays of Cala Vedella and Cala Tarida in the west, and big, brash Platja d'en Bossa in the east; the rest of the shore is more or less pristine. Inland, the rolling, forested countryside is dotted with small, attractive villages. The south is well blessed with dining options, from simple shoreside chiringuitos to swanky country restaurants, as well as being home to some of the island's best beach clubs and bars.

Sant Josep

MAP P.84, POCKET MAP B13
Bus #8 from Ibiza Town and Sant Antoni, all year Mon–Sat (July & Aug daily).
Bus #9 from Sant Antoni and the airport mid-May to mid-Oct daily. Bus #26 from Ibiza Town (destination Cala Vedella) mid-May to mid-Oct daily. Bus #38 from Ibiza Town (destination Cala Tarida) June to mid-Oct daily.

Sant Josep de Sa Talaia

Pretty, prosperous and easy-going **Sant Josep** has a delightful setting, 200m above sea level in a valley overlooked by the green, forested slopes of Sa Talaia. The village itself is of no great size, but it is the main settlement in the region. There's a tidy simplicity to the place, best illustrated along the attractive, pint-sized high street, and around the exquisite little central plaça just to the west, where the Moorish-style tiled benches are shaded by pines. From this plaça you have an excellent view across the main road to the imposing, whitewashed **Església de Sant Josep**, dating from 1726. Eating options abound in Sant Josep, from the simplicity of *Can LLorenç* (see page 93) and traditional tapas at *Destino* (see page 94) to the more exotic Japanese-Peruvian fusion menu at the excellent *Can Limo* (see page 93).

Sant Agustí

MAP P.84, POCKET MAP B12
Bus #8 from Ibiza Town and Sant Antoni, all year Mon–Sat (July & Aug daily). Bus #9 from Sant Antoni and the airport mid-May to mid-Oct daily.

Sa Talaia

About three kilometres north of Sant Josep, the very picturesque hilltop village of **Sant Agustí** is so tranquil that all signs of life seem to have been frazzled by the Mediterranean sun. Grouped around the fortified church at the heart of the settlement are a clump of old farmhouses, one of which has been beautifully converted into the *Can Berri Vell* restaurant; there's also a charming village bar-restaurant *Bar Can Berri* (see page 93), a solitary store and an ancient stone defence tower where the locals once hid from pirates. Captivating views across the hilly interior of the island and down to the southwest coast can be seen from the little plaça next to the landmark **Església de Sant Agustí**, completed in the early nineteenth century.

Sa Talaia

MAP P.84, POCKET MAP B13

Towering above southern Ibiza, the 476-metre peak of **Sa Talaia** is the highest point in the Pitiuses. It's reachable either by a 45-minute waymarked hike from Sant Josep, or a dirt road (also signposted) that turns off the road to Cala Carbó, 2km west of Sant Josep. Thickly wooded with aleppo and Italian stone pines, the summit offers exceptional views of southern Ibiza from gaps between the trees. You should easily be able to pick out the humpback cliffs of Jondal and Falcó, the Salines saltpans and plateau-like Formentera – and on very clear days, the mountains of the Dénia peninsula in mainland Spain, some 50km distant. It's

Arrival and information

Getting around the south is easy with your own vehicle, as there's a decent **road network** and plenty of signposts. **Buses** run along the highway between Sant Antoni and Ibiza Town via Sant Josep, and there are also services to the airport and some beaches (indicated in the text) during the summer.

The south

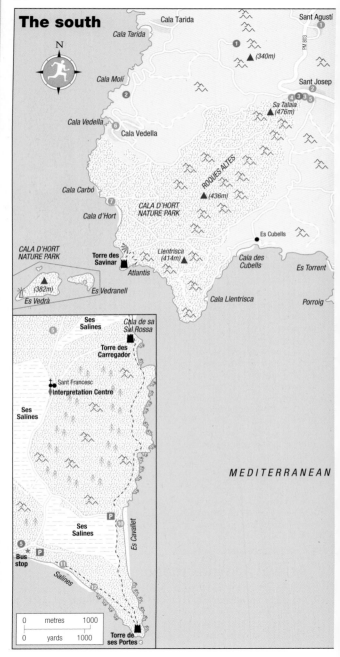

Cala Tarida

Sant Agustí

PM 803

Cala Tarida

N

1

▲ (340m)

Cala Molí

Sant Josep

2

4 3 5

Cala Vedella

6

Cala Vedella

Sa Talaia
▲ (476m)

ROQUES ALTES

Cala Carbó

7

▲ (436m)

CALA D'HORT
NATURE PARK

Cala d'Hort

Es Cubells

CALA D'HORT
NATURE PARK

Llentrisca
(414m) ▲

Torre des
Savinar

Cala des
Cubells

Es Torrent

▲
(382m)

Atlantis

Es Vedrà

Es Vedranell

Cala Llentrisca

Porroig

Ses
Salines

5

Cala de sa
Sal Rossa

Torre des
Carregador

Sant Francesc
Interpretation Centre

Ses
Salines

MEDITERRANEAN

P

Ses
Salines

10

Es Cavallet

5

P

Bus
stop

11

Salines

12

0   metres   1000

0   yards   1000

Torre de
ses Portes

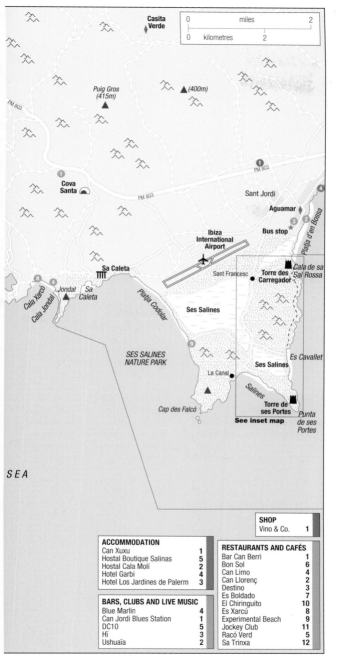

Cala Vedella

wonderfully peaceful here, the
silence broken only by the buzz
of cicadas and hum of a number
of television antennae. In the
1960s, the summit was the scene
of legendary full-moon parties.

Cala Tarida

MAP P.84, POCKET MAP A12
Bus #5 from Sant Antoni, May–Oct daily.
Bus #38 from Ibiza Town June to mid-Oct
daily.

A wide arc of golden sand broken
by two small rocky outcrops, **Cala
Tarida** is home to one of Ibiza's
more appealing resorts, a small,
family-oriented collection of low-
rise hotels surrounding a pretty
bay. In high season, the beach gets
very busy with holidaymakers,
and you'll have to pick your way
through rows of umbrellas and
sunbeds for a swim. There are
plenty of bars and restaurants to
choose from; the best seafood is
served at the expensive *Cas Milà*,
while the best cocktails and sunset
views can be found at *Cotton
Beach Club*.

Cala Molí

MAP P.84, POCKET MAP A13
Two kilometres south of Cala
Tarida, the serpentine coast
road dips down to **Cala Molí**,
a fine beach at the foot of a
seasonal riverbed. Steep cliffs
envelop the pebbly cove, which is
undeveloped except for the French
Mediterranean restaurant *Bagatelle
Beach*. The bay's sheltered, deep-
green waters are very inviting and
great for snorkelling and, if you
swim across to the cove's southern
cliff, you can also explore a small
cave. Cala Molí never seems to
get too busy, probably because it's
not served by buses – if you can
get here independently, you'll find
it's perfect for a chilled-out day by
the sea.

Cala Vedella

MAP P.84, POCKET MAP A13
Bus #26 from Ibiza Town mid-May to
mid-Oct daily.

Continuing south from Cala
Molí, the precipitous, shady road
twists through the coastal pines

for 3km, passing luxury holiday homes before emerging above the long, narrow-mouthed inlet that harbours **Cala Vedella**. One of Ibiza's most attractive and upmarket resorts, its good-quality villas and well-spaced, low-rise hotels are separated into two main developments around the low hills framing the bay. The sheltered, sandy beach is ideal for families, with calm, very shallow water and a collection of snack bars and restaurants backing onto the sands, including the superb *Bon Sol* (see page 93). Paddle Surf Ibiza (Ⓦ paddlesurfibiza.es) operate from here and there's a well-established dive centre (Big Blue, Ⓦ bigblueibiza.com) as well as kayaks and pedalos for hire on the beach.

Cala Carbó

MAP P.84, POCKET MAP A13

A tiny, tranquil cove-bay, **Cala Carbó**, 4km south of Cala Vedella, gets its name from the Catalan word for coal, which was unloaded here until the 1960s. The lovely little sand-and-pebble beach never seems to get too packed and is backed by low sandstone cliffs, and calm, tempting sea; the mossy, rounded boulders offshore lend the water a deep jade tone. Snorkelling is good off the southern shore up to the rocky point at the mouth of the cove, where colourful wrasse and large schools of mirror fish are common. There are two seafood restaurants at the back of the bay serving the usual mix of seafood, rice and meat dishes.

Cala d'Hort

MAP P.84, POCKET MAP A13

Cala d'Hort, 4km south of Cala Carbó, an expansive beach of coarse sand and pebbles, has one of the most spectacular settings in the Balearics. Directly opposite is the startling, vertiginous rock-island of Es Vedrà (see page 87), while the beach is backed by the steep

forested hillsides of the Roques Altes peaks, part of the beautiful **Cala d'Hort Nature Park**. There's a wonderfully isolated feel here, wedged as it is into Ibiza's southwest corner, but despite the remote location, the beach can get pretty busy and if the parking area (free) directly behind the beach is full you'll need to park on the steep access road.

You'll find three good fish restaurants by the shore – the best is *Es Boldado* on the northern lip of the bay (see page 94), while *El Carmen* serves up great paella and fish dishes with more of a relaxed beach-shack vibe but equally impressive views.

Es Vedrà

MAP P.84, POCKET MAP A13

Rising from the sea like the craggy crest of a semi-submerged volcano, the limestone outcrop of **Es Vedrà** is one of the most startling sights in the western Mediterranean. Despite its height (382m), it is only visible once you get within a few kilometres of Cala d'Hort. Legends surround the much-photographed rock, and it's said to be the island of the sirens (the sea nymphs who tried to lure Odysseus from his ship

Cala d'Hort

in Homer's epic), as well as the holy isle of the Carthaginian love and fertility goddess, Tanit. A reclusive Carmelite priest, Father Palau i Quer, reported seeing visions of the Virgin Mary and satanic rituals here in the nineteenth century. Sailors and scuba divers have told of compasses swinging wildly and gauges malfunctioning as they approach the island, and there have been innumerable stories of UFO sightings.

These days, Es Vedrà is inhabited only by a unique subspecies of the Ibizan wall lizard and a small colony of the endangered Eleanor's falcon. Numerous companies offer boat tours around Es Vedrà departing from Sant Antoni, including sunset cruises and glass-bottom boats (see page 127). Ibiza Kayak (@ ibizakayak.es) offer guided kayak trips around the rock (2–3 hours, €50) and/or on to Atlantis (4 hours, €60) departing from Cala d'Hort.

Torre des Savinar
MAP P.84

Two kilometres along the exhilaratingly scenic road from Cala d'Hort to Es Cubells, a right-hand turn-off leads to **Torre des**

Savinar, a defence tower built in 1763 – it's also known (and should be signposted) as Torre d'en Pirata (the pirate tower). The dirt track ends after 500m, where there's a small roundabout and parking area. From here it's a ten-minute walk to the coastal cliffs, where there's an amazing view over the sea to Es Vedrà, particularly at sunset.

From the tower itself there are even better vistas over Vedrà's sister island **Es Vedranell**, which resembles a sleeping dragon, its snout and spiky backbone protruding from the water.

Atlantis
MAP P.84

Directly below the Torre des Savinar you can make out the outline of **Atlantis**, an ancient shoreside quarry some 200m down. To get there, retrace your steps to the parking area and take another path that sets off to the right (east); you'll quickly reach the clifftop trailhead, from where Atlantis is a 30-minute hike away. The very steep, slippery, well-trodden path down the cliff side is directly in front of you when you reach the clifftop; it's not immediately visible until you're standing near the cliff

Torre des Savinar

edge. Once located, the path is easy to follow; wherever it seems to split, keep to the right. It flattens out after fifteen minutes beside a small **cave**, where there's a beautiful etched image of a Buddha, said to have been drawn by a Japanese traveller.

From the cave, you have to plough your way through sand dunes, but as you near the shore, the hewn forms of the ancient quarry – set at oblique angles from the bedrock – become clear. The stone here was used in the construction of Ibiza Town's magnificent walls.

Between the rock outcrops, shimmering indigo- and emerald-tinged pools of trapped seawater add an ethereal dimension to the scene. Much of the stone has been carved by hippies with mystic imagery – blunt-nosed faces resembling Maya gods, swirling abstract doodles and graffiti – while blocks of stone hang suspended by wires from the rock face. At the edge of the promontory there's a wonderful, partly painted carving of a Cleopatra-like queen. Bring plenty of water, sun cream and a sun hat, as there's no shade.

Es Cubells

MAP P.84

South of Sant Josep, a signposted road weaves around the eastern flank of Sa Talaia, past terraces of orange and olive trees, to the southern coast and the tiny cliffside village of **Es Cubells**. The settlement owes its place on the map to Father Palau i Quer, a

Es Cubells

Carmelite priest who saw visions of the Virgin Mary on nearby Es Vedrà in the 1850s, and who persuaded the Vatican to construct a chapel here in 1855 for the local farmers and fishermen. Magnificently positioned above the Mediterranean, and with stunning views down to the turquoise waters below, the simple whitewashed sandstone church is the focal point of the hamlet. To the right of the church, *Bar Llumbi* is a simple seafood bar-restaurant ideal for lunch with a view.

Cala Llentrisca

MAP P.84

Southwest of Es Cubells, the road hugs the eastern slopes of the Llentrisca headland, descending for

Platja d'en Bossa hike

It's possible to hike from Platja d'en Bossa to Es Cavallet along an easy-to-follow shady path that trails the coastline, passing rocky coves and pine forests. From the extreme southernmost part of Platja d'en Bossa beach head to the sixteenth-century **Torre des Carregador**, a defence tower just above the beach, and continue to the south. The hike takes about an hour and thirty minutes and doesn't stray more than 50m or so from the sea.

Salines saltpans

Ibiza's spectacular saltpans, which stretch across 435 hectares in the south of the island, were its only reliable source of wealth for more than 2000 years. The Phoenicians first developed the land and, although other invaders continued to maintain the saltpans, it was the Moors, experts at hydraulic technology, who developed the water channels still in use today. Each May approximately 2500 cubic metres of seawater is left to evaporate, forming a ten-centimetre crust of pinky-white powder that is scooped up and amassed in huge salt hills, of which around 50,000 tonnes are exported annually. The pans are part of the Ses Salines Nature Park and an important habitat for **birds**. Storks, herons and flamingos stop to rest and refuel at what is one of the first points of call on the migratory route from Africa, while over 200 species are in permanent residence. To find out more, visit the Interpretation Centre next to the church in Sant Francesc (May–Oct Wed–Sun 10am–2pm & 6–9pm, Nov–April Sat & Sun 10am–2pm; free), who also provide binoculars and a viewing platform. Ibiza salt products are available in shops around the island and from Sal de Ibiza outlets (see page 52).

3km past luxurious modern villas towards the lovely, unspoilt cove of **Cala Llentrisca**, cut off from the rest of the island by soaring pine-clad slopes. You'll need your own transport to get here; when the guard stops you at the barrier, say 'Cala Llentrisca' then continue along the coastal road. Park beside the final villa at the end of the road and walk the last ten minutes along a rugged path over the headland to the beach. Bear in mind that there's very little shade, and nothing on the pebbly shoreline except a row of seldom-used fishing huts and a lot of compressed seaweed, with a yacht or two often moored in the translucent waters.

Cala Jondal

MAP P.84, POCKET MAP B13
Bus #26 from Ibiza Town and Sant Josep, mid-May to mid-Oct daily.
The broad pebble beach of **Cala Jondal** lies between the promontories of Porroig and Jondal some 9km southeast of Sant Josep. A stony seashore at the base of terraces planted with fruit trees, Jondal's kilometre-long strip

of pebbles and imported sand doesn't make one of the island's finest swimming spots. It's for its beach clubs that Cala Jondal is famous, namely the iconic *Blue Marlin* (see page 96), its sister restaurant *Yemanjá*, as well as the more relaxed *Tropicana Beach Club* (April–Oct daily, Ⓦ tropicanaibiza.com).

If you're coming from Cala Xarcó, Cala Jondal is a couple of minutes' scramble over the cliff behind *Es Xarcú* (see page 94); you can also drive via a precipitous dirt road from the beach – after 200m, take the first right beside some walled villas.

Sa Caleta

MAP P.84
Bus #26 from Ibiza Town and Sant Josep, mid-May to mid-Oct daily.
Four kilometres around the coast from Cala Jondal lie the **ruins** of **Sa Caleta**, the first Phoenician settlement in Ibiza. Established around 650 BC, the small site was only occupied for about fifty years, before the Phoenicians moved to the site of what is now

Ibiza Town. Today, a high metal fence surrounds the foundations of the village, once home to several hundred people, who lived by fishing, hunting and farming wheat. The ruins are visually unimpressive, but the site is a peaceful place to visit, with expansive views over an azure sea towards Platja Codolar and Cap des Falcó.

Just west of the site are Sa Caleta's **beaches**, three tiny adjoining bays sometimes labelled as "Es Bol Nou" on maps. The first bay, a hundred-metre strip of coarse golden sand, is the busiest spot, and very popular with Ibizan families at weekends – there are some sunbeds and umbrellas to rent here in summer, excellent swimming and snorkelling, and the well-regarded *Restaurante Sa Caleta*. The other two bays, both secluded and pebbly, are to the west of the sandy bay, via a path that winds along the shore below Sa Caleta's low sandstone cliffs.

Casita Verde

MAP P.84
11km northwest of Sant Josep ☎ 971 187 353, ⓦ greenheart.org/casita-verde
Enjoying a wonderful location in a remote valley between Sant Josep and Sant Rafel, **Casita Verde** is a model ecology centre demonstrating sustainable living in a fun and educational way. Electricity is mostly generated by solar and wind power and water-saving and recycling techniques are fundamental to the project. There's plenty to investigate, including structures made from bottles and cans, and fields of aloe vera and carob trees. Casita Verde is run by volunteers and is open to visitors each Sunday from 2–7pm when they provide a vegetarian lunch (till 4pm, €7, registration required) made from locally-sourced ingredients, followed by a tour of the centre. Check the website for directions.

Platja d'en Bossa

MAP P.84, POCKET MAP C13
Bus #14 from Ibiza Town, all year daily, plus hourly night buses June–Sept. Bus #36 from the airport end June to mid-Sept daily. Bus #11B from Ibiza Town (destination Ses Salines) May–Sept daily. Bus #3B from Sant Antoni (via Ibiza Town) end June to mid-Sept daily. Boat from Passeig Marítim, May–Oct daily.
Merging into Figueretes to the north (see page 37) and Ibiza Town beyond, the cheap(ish) and cheerful resort of **Platja d'en Bossa** is stretched out along the island's longest beach – a ruler-straight, three-kilometre-long strip of wonderfully fine, pale sand. Lining the beach are a gap-toothed row of hotel blocks, many abruptly thrown up in the later Franco years and others still in various stages of construction; behind these lies a secondary strip of pizza, kebab and burger joints, pop-up stalls selling club and boat tickets and minimarkets filled with plastic dolphins, cigarettes and sun cream.

Despite the tourist tat, Platja d'en Bossa is popular as a base for savvy older clubbers who have tired of the San An scene and

Casita Verde

stay here to take advantage of the location – it's home to some of the island's big hitters, including *Ushuaïa* and *Hi* (see page 97), and only a few kilometres from both Ibiza Town and the sands at Ses Salines. It's also popular with families, who take advantage of the beach's many watersports, including the swimming pool and water slides at Aguamar Water Park (June–Sept, 10am–6pm). The main drawbacks are the lack of decent restaurants, most of which serve bland "international" food, and the constant stream of aeroplanes that thunder overhead.

Es Cavallet

MAP P.84, POCKET MAP C14

Franco's Guardia Civil fought a futile battle against nudism on this stunning beach for years, arresting hundreds of naked hippies before the kilometre-long stretch of sand was finally designated Ibiza's first naturist shore in 1978. The northern end of the beach, close to *El Chiringuito* restaurant (see page 94) and the car park, attracts a mixed bunch of families and couples, but the southern half of the beach – the nicest stretch – is almost exclusively gay, centred around the superb *Chiringay* bar-café.

Platja Codolar

MAP P.84, POCKET MAP C13

East of Sa Caleta, a road runs parallel to the ochre-coloured coastal cliffs, heading towards the airport and Ibiza Town. Just before the airport, there's a turn-off for **Platja Codolar**, a sweeping pebble beach that stretches for over 3km southeast, running close to the airport runway and skirting the fringes of the Salines saltpans. Even at the height of summer, there are rarely more than a dozen or so sunbathers here, and the place would be very peaceful were it not for the regular interruption of jet engines. It's also possible to get to

the opposite end of Platja Codolar via the main road to Salines beach; follow the signs for restaurant-beach club *Experimental Beach* (see page 94) at Cap des Falcó.

Salines beach

MAP P.84

Bus #11 from Ibiza Town, May–Oct daily; Nov–April Mon, Wed & Fri. Bus #11B from Ibiza Town, May–Sept daily.

A beautiful kilometre-long strip of powdery sand backed by pines and dunes, **Salines beach** is one of Ibiza's most popular places to pose. In the height of summer the sands here are thick with sun-worshippers, whose attention is vied for by a steady stream of club promotors and refreshment vendors. Some great bars dot the shoreline, including premier beach-restaurant *Jockey Club* (see page 95) and the uber-hip *Sa Trinxa chiringuito* (see page 95), where sunbathing nude is the norm.

Beyond *Sa Trinxa* are a succession of tiny sandy coves, enveloped by unusual rock formations. These mini-beaches tend to get grabbed fairly early in the day and jealously guarded as private bays by dedicated – and pretty territorial – sunbathers.

Punta de ses Portes

MAP P.84, POCKET MAP C14

A fifteen-minute walk south from Es Cavallet beach is Ibiza's most southerly point, **Punta de ses Portes**, a lonely, rocky spot, often lashed by winds and waves. Above the swirling currents is a two-storey, sixteenth-century defence tower, **Torre de ses Portes**, which commands superb views of the chain of tiny islands, topped by lighthouses, that reach out to Formentera. One of these, Illa des Penjats (Island of the Hanged), was used for executions while another, Illa des Porcs (Pig Island), was once a pig-smugglers' stronghold.

Shop

Vino & Co.

MAP P.84

Ctra. Sant Antoni 60, Can Bellotera, Sant Jordi. ☎ 971 305 324. ⓦ vinoyco. com. Mon–Fri 10am–2pm & 5–8pm, Sat 10am–2pm.

Wine shop specializing in wines from smaller, lesser-known Spanish and international bodegas. Especially popular for their wine and tapas nights on Wed & Fri in winter when the shop stays open late. Wine by the glass and some selected tapas also available throughout the summer season, but only during shop hours.

Restaurants and cafés

Bar Can Berri

MAP P.84

Plaça Major 3, Sant Agustí. ☎ 971 803 035, ⓦ barcanberri.com. May to mid-Oct Tues–Sun 6pm–12.30am (Aug open daily), mid-Oct to Nov closed, Dec–Apr Fri–Sun noon–midnight.

Occupying prime position in one of Ibiza's prettiest villages, *Bar Can Berri* is also a very decent restaurant with a charming garden courtyard where you can dine under orange and lemon trees. Every other Sunday during Feb–April, one of Ibiza's best winter events, the *calçotada*, is celebrated here, when the whole garden area is opened up and barbecued *calçots* (like large spring onions) are served accompanied by live music and much merriment.

Bon Sol

MAP P.84

On the beach front at Cala Vedella. ☎ 971 808 213. April–end Oct 1pm–midnight.

Beachside restaurant offering superb Italian food, gorgeous views over Vedella bay and one of the best sunset vantage points in Ibiza.

The tagliatelle with courgette and prawns is a firm favourite (€14.50) but all the pasta dishes (spelt available) are delicious.

Can Limo

MAP P.84

Ctra. Sant Josep km 12.5, Sant Josep. ☎ 971 800 550, ⓦ canlimoibiza.com. June–Sept Mon & Wed–Sun 7.30pm–12.30am; March–May, Nov & Dec Fri–Sun 8pm–midnight, Sat & Sun 1.30–4.30pm.

Creative and original Peruvian/Asian fusion restaurant. With a regularly changing but constantly appealing menu (sea bass and prawn ceviche, €18, tender beef green curry, €15), it's worth several repeat visits.

Can Llorenç

MAP P.84

C/ Can Pau s/n, Sant Josep. ☎ 971 801 601. Daily 6am–11pm.

Simple café-bar opposite the church in Sant Josep village whose homemade churros con chocolate are the main reason to visit – only served on Sundays from 8am–midday (€2 full portion, €1 half, chocolate with cinnamon €1.60 extra). At other times, it's still a

Vino & Co.

Vino & Co.

great place to hang like a local and eat excellent tostadas and montaditos topped with serrano ham, cheese or omelette for just a few euros.

Destino

MAP P.84

C/ Atalaya 15, Sant Josep. ☎ 971 800 341. End April–Oct Mon–Sat 1pm–1am.

This fine, intimate place is famous for its tapas, which are inventively prepared and inexpensively priced, from €6, with plenty of choice for vegetarians. There's a small pavement terrace and a comfortable dining room. Book ahead on summer nights.

Es Boldado

MAP P.84

Cala d'Hort. ☎ 626 494 537 (mobile). May–Sept daily 1–5pm & 7.30–11.30pm, Oct & Feb–April daily 1–5pm, Nov–Jan closed.

Overlooking Es Vedrà, this seafood restaurant boasts a stunning location, particularly at sunset. The menu offers superb paella, fish stew

and their speciality, Es Boldado black rice (min. 2pp, €22pp) as well as a long list of homemade desserts from €6. You can drive to *Es Boldado* via a signposted side road just northwest of Cala d'Hort (C/ Cala Vedella), or it's a 5min walk west of the same beach, past the fishermen's huts.

El Chiringuito

MAP P.84

Playa Es Cavallet. ☎ 971 395 355, Ⓦ elchiringuitoibiza.com. April to mid–Oct daily 10am–midnight.

A classy beachside café-restaurant which serves everything from breakfast, coffees and cocktails to full meals. The lengthy menu features gourmet beef burgers (€24), spaghetti frutti di mare (€60 for two) and a sublime lobster risotto (€39) which you can enjoy on the terrace facing the waves.

Es Xarcú

MAP P.84

Cala es Xarcó. ☎ 971 187 867, Ⓦ esxarcurestaurante.com. June–Aug 1–11pm, May, Sept & Oct 1–10pm.

Like many seafood restaurants in Ibiza, this beachside place looks very humble, with rickety tables and chairs, but the quality of the cooking, freshness of the fish and size of the bill defy appearances. The signature dish here is the baked *pez de San Pedro* (wild Atlantic John Dory, €80 per kilo), which is cooked in a butter-rich white-wine sauce and served in traditional style with potatoes and peppers. It's not an easy place to find, but best approached from Es Torrent – the yachts offshore are a giveaway that a lot of the diners arrive by boat.

Experimental Beach

MAP P.84

Platja Codolar, Ses Salines. ☎ 664 331 269, Ⓦ eccbeach.com. April–Oct daily 10am–2am.

El Chiringuito

Jockey Club

Elegant restaurant-beach club in a unique setting on Platja Codolar – follow the signs from Salines along a narrow dirt track across the salt pans. Famous for its cocktails – try the Belza gin infused with pink peppercorns, orange blossom and cucumber, €14 – and spectacular sunsets. Gets very busy, but there's nothing to stop you bringing your own towel/cushion and enjoying the music and ambience from the surrounding rocks.

Jockey Club

MAP P.84

Platja de ses Salines. ☏ 971 395 788, ⓦ jockeyclubibiza.com. April–Nov daily 9am–10pm, Dec–March Fri–Sun & holidays 11am–6pm.

With a great location on Salines beach, this fun restaurant-*chiringuito* serves homemade pizzas (from €18) as well as a wide range of other mains, including seabass and prawn ceviche (€27) and delicious Khao Soi (red chicken curry, €27), plus cocktails from €12. DJs play every day from 2–8pm and things can get pretty lively late afternoon. Best to reserve in high season.

Racó Verd

MAP P.84

Plaça de l'Església, Sant Josep. ☏ 971 800 267, ⓦ racoverdibiza.es. April–Sept Mon–Sat 10am–3am; Oct–March Thurs–Sat 6pm–late.

There is nightly live music at this bar-restaurant whose outdoor terrace boasts a 1000-year-old olive tree. Music (from 10pm) varies nightly from rock to world music and flamenco. The café-bar serves Mexican food such as tacos and quesadillas as well as wraps, salads and a variety of fruits juices (from €5) and cocktails.

Sa Trinxa

MAP P.84

Platja de ses Salines. ☏ 618 960 500, ⓦ satrinxa.com. April–Oct daily 11am–10pm.

The definitive Ibizan party *chiringuito*, set at the southern end of Ses Salines. Outstanding, eclectic mixes courtesy of daily resident DJs are beamed out to the assorted supine Balearic wildlife: club faces, models and wannabes, party freaks and Euro slackers. Meals are served, but the burgers, stir-fries and *bocadillos* are some of the priciest in Ibiza. Gets very busy, especially around sundown.

Bars, clubs and live music

Blue Marlin

MAP P.84
Cala Jondal s/n. ☎ 971 410 269, ⓦ bluemarlinibiza.com. May–Sept daily 11am–4am.

An Ibiza pioneer in its day, *Blue Marlin* was and still is the ultimate Balearic beach club. Elegant white sun loungers spread out along the soft sands of Cala Jondal, the shaded dining area serves modern Mediterranean cuisine (Wagyu ribeye steak, €19 per 100g, langostine, king crab and dover sole, €48), and DJs play every day until 4am. Sunday is the star day, when things get particularly lively, while Friday's 'Pop-u-Up' is a heady mix of urban street art, house music and performance artists. Free entry but early reservation of sun beds and loungers is essential.

Can Jordi Blues Station

MAP P.84
Ctra. Sant Josep–Ibiza km 8. ☎ 971 800 182. Mon–Sat 7am–10pm.

If you need a break from Balearic beats and bling, this place serves up good ol' fashioned rock and roll to a local, boisterous crowd seated outdoors in what would otherwise be a car park. Despite humble appearances, the atmosphere on Friday nights and Saturday afternoons, when live bands play, most of whom are local to the island, is electric. Music starts at 8.30pm on Fridays and at 4.30pm on summer Saturdays (2pm in winter).

DC10

MAP P.84
Ctra. Ses Salines, km 1, Ses Salines. ⓦ dc10-ibiza.ibiza-clubs.net. June–Oct. Entrance €20–40.

This scruffy club has a raw, unpretentious appeal that's completely different to the more corporate-minded venues. Forgoing commerce for pure party spirit, it's famed for its underground vibe and all-day after parties, though it offers some night-time club action too. The venue is located in a rural corner of Ibiza, a stone's throw from the airport. The covered terrace, where all the action takes place, is little more than a wall around a paved floor, topped by a roof to mask the noise of planes taking off, and bordered by the giant reeds of neighbouring fields. A long-term favourite for serious hedonists into electro music.

Hï

MAP P.84
Platja d'en Bossa Ⓦ **hiibiza.com. May–Oct. Entrance €45–50.**
Occupying the space formally occupied by Space, a tough act to follow in Ibiza club land. But with a state of the art renovation, two main rooms, three outdoor areas, stunning light shows and even a DJ booth in the toilets, plus a new set every night and an events calendar featuring the full spectrum of electronic music, it's already making its mark. Popular parties include Glitterbox on Fridays and Hï Sundays.

Ushuaïa

MAP P.84
Platja d'en Bossa 10. Ⓦ **ushuaiabeachhotel. com. May–Oct. Entrance €40–60.**
A firm fixture on the Ibiza club scene famous for big names, daytime clubbing, a gorgeous pool area and extraordinary stage productions. It manages to attract some of the biggest names each year, including David Guetta and ANTS. Opens around 4pm and closes at midnight.

CIROC Party at Ushuaïa

Formentera

Tranquil, easy-going Formentera could hardly be more of a contrast to Ibiza. The island is very flat, consisting of two shelf-like plateaux connected by a narrow central isthmus, and has a population of just 12,000. Most visitors are drawn here by the exceptionally clear water and some of the longest, whitest, cleanest and least crowded beaches in Spain. The island has just one resort, Es Pujols, a restrained, small-scale affair, with the pick of the beaches close by. Inland, the beautiful, sun-baked countryside is a patchwork of golden wheatfields, vines, carob and fig trees, divided by old dry-stone walls. Of the three villages, the central, diminutive capital, Sant Francesc Xavier, is the most interesting, while the island's extremes – where you'll find lonely lighthouses and stunning coastal scenery – are captivating.

La Savina

MAP P.100

Set in a small natural harbour in the northwest corner of the island, orderly **La Savina** is likely to be your first view of Formentera, as all ferries from Ibiza dock here. Never more than a minor settlement for the export of salt and planks of sabina pine (from which it takes its name), it's still a sleepy place today, ferry traffic aside. While not that absorbing, the modern harbour is pleasant enough, and the souvenir shops and cafés are perfectly placed if you need to while away an hour or so before your ferry departs.

La Savina harbour

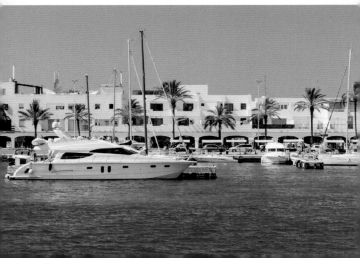

Es Campament

MAP P.100

On the eastern edge of La Savina, just south of the highway, the concentration camp of **Es Campament** housed several hundred prisoners-of-war and anti-Francoists in the years following the Spanish Civil War. Very little remains today, except some walls entwined with barbed wire, a ruined meeting hall and a plaque bearing a poem in Catalan by local writer Joan Puig, but an eerie presence still lingers.

Estany Pudent and Estany des Peix

MAP P.100, POCKET MAP C15
Buses on the La Savina–La Mola highway pass within 300m of both lakes.

Formentera's two **salt lakes**, the island's main wetland habitats and part of the Parc Natural de Ses Salines, are just to the south of La Savina. On the left, **Estany Pudent**, or "Stinking Pond", is the larger of the two. Ringed by scrub bush and an unsightly jumble of bungalows, it's not exactly pretty, but is popular amongst birdwatchers, who come to see herons and egret,

Estany Pudent and Estany des Peix

black-necked grebe, warbler and even the odd flamingo. Dirt tracks run around the entire lake; you can get to the shoreline via a left-hand turn-off 500m along the main highway from La Savina, signposted Es Pujols and Platja Illetes, which passes through a small patch of saltpans.

Arrival and information

Most visitors choose to get around Formentera independently, and renting transport is easy (see page 124). Maps of the Green Route network of **cycle paths** are available from tourist offices and online (see ⓦ formentera.es) and you can rent bikes (see page 125). The island also has a pretty reasonable **bus network**, with daily services operating a loop around the main settlements between May and October, plus buses to Far de la Mola and Platja Illetes. Services are much reduced for the rest of the year, see ⓦ busformentera.com for full timetables. Several companies run **ferries** and **hydrofoils** between Ibiza Town and La Savina (see page 122) and boat operators in most Ibiza resorts offer **day-trips** to Formentera.

There's a **tourist information** office just behind the harbour in La Savina (Mon–Fri 10am–2pm & 5–7pm, Sat 10am–2pm; ☏ 971 321 210) plus one in Sant Francesc (Plaça Constitucio s/n, May–Oct Mon–Sat 10am–2pm & 6–8pm; Nov–Apr Mon–Sat 10am–1.30pm).

FORMENTERA

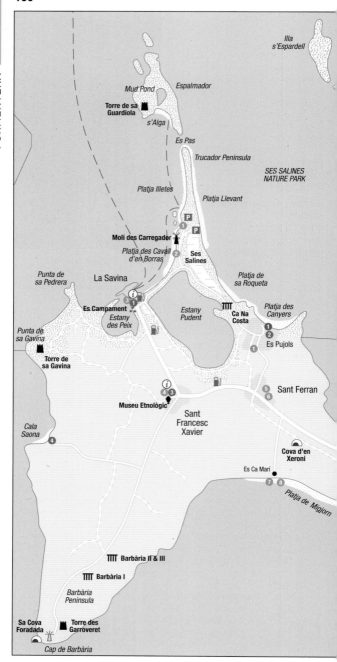

Formentera

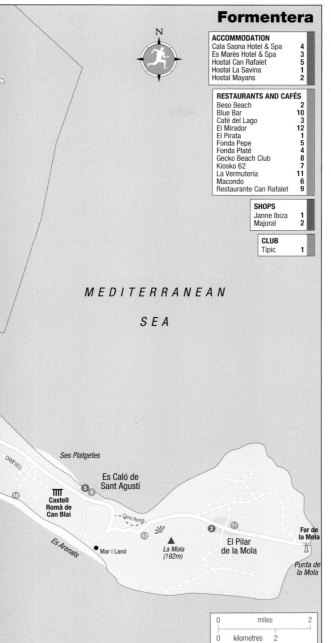

ACCOMMODATION

Cala Saona Hotel & Spa	4
Es Marès Hotel & Spa	3
Hostal Can Rafalet	5
Hostal La Savina	1
Hostal Mayans	2

RESTAURANTS AND CAFÉS

Beso Beach	2
Blue Bar	10
Café del Lago	3
El Mirador	12
El Pirata	1
Fonda Pepe	5
Fonda Platé	4
Gecko Beach Club	8
Kiosko 62	7
La Vermutería	11
Macondo	6
Restaurante Can Rafalet	9

SHOPS

Janne Ibiza	1
Majoral	2

CLUB

Tipic	1

N

MEDITERRANEAN

SEA

CAMÍ VELL

Ses Platgetes

Es Caló de
Sant Agustí

🏛 Castell
Romà de
Can Blai

Camí Romà

Es Arenals

Mar i Land

La Mola
(192m)

El Pilar
de la Mola

Far de
la Mola

Punta de
la Mola

0	miles	2
0	kilometres	2

Smaller **Estany des Peix**, to the right of the highway via a turn-off 1km south of La Savina signposted Porto/Salè, has a narrow mouth to the sea, and its shallow waters act as an ideal nursery for young fish. The brackish lagoon is no more picturesque than its neighbour, and not as rich birding territory, but there are plenty of terns and ducks and you may encounter the odd wader.

Sant Francesc Xavier

MAP P.100, POCKET MAP C15
Buses #1 & #2 from La Savina, mid-May to Oct daily; Nov to mid-May Mon–Sat.

Formentera's tiny capital, **Sant Francesc Xavier**, 2km southeast of La Savina, is a pretty little town with an attractive network of whitewashed streets. Its heart is the Plaça de sa Constitució, a fetching little square with a few benches scattered between gnarled olive trunks and palm trees. Consecrated in 1726, the forbidding, fortified **Església de Sant Francesc Xavier** stands on the north side of the plaça, its stark plastered facade embellished only with a tiny window set high in the wall.

Adjoining the church to the south is the unpretentious, blue-shuttered old government building, while on the opposite side of the square, its attractive modern replacement, the **Casa de sa Constitució**, was built from local sandstone.

By Formentera's standards, Sant Francesc gets quite lively in summer when it bustles with tourists making the most of the shops and bars that have cropped up to cater to them. On Saturday evenings, live jazz plays in the plaça and there's outdoor cinema on Tuesday evenings at the Jardí de ses Eres. Sant Francesc's market is held Mon–Sat from 10am–2pm during May–Oct.

Museu Etnològic

MAP P.100
C/ Sant Jaume I, Sant Francesc. Mon–Fri 9.30am–2pm & 4–7pm. Free.

Sant Francesc's modest **Museu Etnològic**, situated above a little cultural centre, has a moderately interesting collection of highly polished old farming tools and fishing gear. There are also a few curious old photographs of the island, including one from the early

Museu Etnològic

Salines saltpans

Formentera's shimmering saltpans lie at the very top of the island. They haven't been in commercial use since 1984, but crystallization in the steely-blue pools continues nevertheless, with foam-like clusters of salt clinging to the fringes of the low stone walls that divide the pans.

As an extension to Estany Pudent and Estany des Peix, the saltpans form an important wetland zone, attracting gulls, terns, waders and flamingoes. The pans and surrounding coastal region of northern Formentera, as well as southern Ibiza and Espalmador, are included within the protected **Parc Natural de Ses Salines**.

twentieth century of a very muddy, desolate-looking Sant Francesc. Outside the museum is the tiny toy-town steam train that used to shunt the island's salt to the docks from the saltpans.

Cala Saona

MAP P.100, POCKET MAP C16
Bus #5 from Sant Francesc, May–Oct daily.
South of Sant Francesc, an undulating, ruler-straight main road runs for 2.5km to a signposted branch road that veers west through rust-red fields of carob and fig, and small coppices of aleppo pine, to the appealing bay of **Cala Saona**, 3km from the junction. The only cove beach in Formentera (and a busy spot in summer), Cala Saona has temptingly turquoise water and fine sand that extends 100m back from the coast to the excellent hotel-restaurant *Cala Saona* (see page 118).

Centro Náutico Formentera (June–Oct 10am–8pm) rent kayaks and SUP boards for €10 an hour from a shack on the beach. The beach is also served by a handful of bar-restaurants, plus the wonderfully placed *chiringuito Cala Saona* (summer daily 10am–10pm, cash only) overlooking the bay. The menu is limited and seating is sparse but the elevated position provides enviable sunset views.

There are some excellent cliffside walking routes south of here, along coastal paths that meander past sabina pines and sand dunes and offer plenty of quiet, shady spots for a picnic lunch. The views from this section of the coast are stunning, with a dramatic perspective over the Mediterranean to the sphinx-like contours of Es Vedrà and Es Vedranell, and to the soaring hills of southern Ibiza; on exceptionally clear days you can make out the jagged mountains around Dénia on the mainland.

Barbària peninsula ruins

MAP P.100
Continuing south from the Cala Saona turn-off, the road gradually begins its ascent of the sparsely populated Barbària peninsula. Along the route there are a collection of minor archeological sites, all signposted from the road. First are the ruined, fenced-off remnants of the 3800-year-old Bronze Age **Barbària II**, which contained nine simple limestone buildings – bedrooms, workrooms, a kiln and animal quarters.

The other sets of remains, **Barbària III** and **Barbària I**, also date from the Bronze Age. Barbària III's singularly unremarkable buildings may have been animal pens while Barbària I consists of a three-metre-wide circular formation of upended stone blocks that may have represented a place of worship, although practically nothing is known about their significance.

Cap de Barbària

MAP P.100

The southernmost point in the Pitiuses forms an eerily beautiful, almost lunar landscape. This isolated region, the **Cap de Barbària**, or "Barbary Cape", is named after the North African pirates who passed this way to plunder the Balearics. The bleak, sun-bleached landscape, dotted with tiny green patches of hardy rosemary and thyme, boasted a dense pine wood until the 1930s, when ruined emigrés, returning to a jobless Formentera during the American Depression, chopped down the trees to make charcoal.

At the end of the road a white-painted lighthouse, the **Far des Barbària**, stands above the swirling, cobalt-blue waters of the Mediterranean. If you pick your way 100m south of the lighthouse, you'll find a cave, **Sa Cova Foradada**, which is worth a quick look. You enter by lowering yourself into a small hole in the roof of the modest single chamber

Església de Sant Ferran

via a ladder; once you're inside, you can edge your way to the mouth of the cave, almost 100m above the sea, for a stunning view of the Mediterranean. The *cova* features in the film *Sex and Lucia*, which was shot in Formentera.

Northeast of the lighthouse, it's a ten-minute walk over to **Torre des Garroveret**, a well-preserved, two-storey eighteenth-century tower. As Formentera's first line of defence against Barbary pirates, it would have been manned night and day in centuries past, but is no longer open.

Note the road gets progressively narrower as you approach the lighthouse, eventually becoming single lane with only rocky laybys for passing. The resulting traffic congestion, particularly bad at sunset in July & Aug, has been controlled to some extent by paid parking restrictions, but once the parking area is full you will be asked to turn back.

Sant Ferran

MAP P.100, POCKET MAP D15
Buses #1 & #2 from La Savina, mid-May to Oct daily; Nov to mid-May Mon–Sat.
Strung out along a busy junction on the main La Savina–La Mola highway, **Sant Ferran**, Formentera's second largest town, has an abundance of banks, bars, stores and restaurants. With its two main streets plagued by traffic noise, first impressions are not great. But the most attractive part of town, hidden away a couple of streets northeast of the main highway, is well worth investigating, centred around the pleasantly austere village church, **Església de Sant Ferran**.

Opposite the church is a spacious, paved **plaça**, lined with seats and palm trees. There's barely a soul to be seen here for most of the year, but in summer things liven up considerably, particularly on Friday evenings when live rock, indie, reggae and Latin American music is played in the square (8pm–midnight). There's music on Tuesdays too, plus an artisanal market (daily except Wed

Es Pujols beach

& Sun) and outdoor cinema on Thursdays (often in original English) but Friday night is party night when the exuberant crowd stretches down from the plaça to the pedestrianised area around bar-hostal *Fonda Pepe* (see page 110).

Es Pujols

MAP P.100, POCKET MAP D15

Bus #1 from La Savina, mid-May to Oct daily; Nov to mid-May Mon–Sat. Bus #3 from La Savina, May–Oct daily; Bus #7 from Illetes, May–Oct daily.

Formentera's only designated resort, **Es Pujols**, 2km north of Sant Ferran, is an attractive, small-scale affair. It's lively but not too boisterous, with a decent quota of bars and a decent nightclub (see page 111). Curving off to the northwest, in front of the clump of hotels and apartment blocks, is the reason why virtually everyone is here: the **beach** – two crescents of fine white sand, separated by a low rocky coastal shelf and dotted with ramshackle fishing huts. The beautiful shallow, turquoise water here heats up to tropical temperatures by August, when it can get very crowded, with rows of sunbeds packing the sands.

There's nothing much to see away from the beach, and most visitors spend the evening wandering along the promenade, selecting a seafront restaurant and browsing the market stalls.

Platja des Cavall d'en Borràs

MAP P.100

Bus #3 from La Savina (Platja Illetes stop), May–Oct daily.

Just west of the saltpans, the slender sandy beach of **Cavall d'en Borràs** (sometimes called Cala Savina) has an excellent but pricey beach club (see page 110), great swimming and wonderful views over to Ibiza and Es Vedrà. Just north of the beach, along a sandy track, there's a huge old windmill, the Molí des Carregador, which used to pump seawater into the saltpans – it's now been converted into a mediocre but expensive seafood restaurant.

Platja Illetes

MAP P.100

Bus #3 from La Savina, May–Oct daily.

From the Molí des Carregador, a sandy track heads north through steep sand dunes and eventually

Platja Illetes

reaches a large car park. Just offshore are the small islets that give this slim stretch of beach its name: **Platja Illetes**. In high season, the sands here are very popular with day-trippers from Ibiza, and with good reason. The astonishingly clear water is normally pancake calm with stunning views over to Ibiza. A handful of bar-restaurants are scattered along the beach, of which the best, at least for location and atmosphere, is *El Pirata* (see page 110).

Such is the popularity of Illetes, parking restrictions apply and from mid-May to end Sept the charge is €6 per car (€4 per motorbike) to drive beyond the windmill. Once the car parks are full, no more vehicles can enter, although it's possible to park beforehand and walk or cycle in.

Platja Llevant
MAP P.100, POCKET MAP C15
Bus #3 from La Savina, May–Oct daily.
Continuing on the sandy track beyond the Platja Illetes car park, the road twists around the tip of the saltpans eastwards to the parking area for **Platja Llevant.** Rivalling its west coast sister in terms of eye-dazzling white sand and turquoise-tinged waters, this glorious undeveloped beach is usually a touch less crowded.

Trucador Peninsula
MAP P.100, POCKET MAP C15
A slender finger of low-lying land, the idyllic **Trucador Peninsula** extends north from Platja Illetes and Llevant towards the island of Espalmador. You'll have to continue on foot if you want to explore this very narrow final section of the peninsula, which is barely 30m wide and bordered by blinding white powdery sand that never seems to get too busy.

A kilometre from the Platja Llevant car park, you reach the northerly tip of Formentera, **Es Pas**, or "The Crossing", partially connected to the island of Espalmador by a 300-metre sand bar. If the sea is not too choppy, you should be able to wade across without soaking your belongings.

Espalmador
MAP P.100, POCKET MAP C14
A shelf-like island of dunes and sandstone rock, most people visit

Espalmador for stunning **S'Alga beach**, with its sublime, shallow water and fine arc of white sand. In summer, the sheltered bay bristles with yachts, and is a favoured destination for day-trippers from Ibiza (many of the Formentera-bound boat-trips from Ibiza stop here on their way to La Savina). Some visitors take time out to visit the **sulphurous mud pond** a few minutes' walk north of the beach.

Platja de Migjorn

MAP P.100, POCKET MAP D16
Bus #2 from La Savina, mid-May to Oct daily; Nov to mid-May Mon–Sat. Bus #3 from La Savina, May–Oct daily. Bus #7 from Illetes, May–Oct daily.

Vying with Platja Illetes for status as Formentera's finest beach, **Platja de Migjorn** is a wonderful six-kilometre swathe of pale sand washed by gleaming, azure water, extending along the entire south coast of Formentera's central strip. Most of it is more or less pristine, with development confined to the extremities – **Es Ca Marí** to the west and Mar i Land (see p.108) to the east. To get to the best stretch of sand, turn south off the highway at the 8km marker, signposted Platja Migjorn and *Blue Bar* (see page 109).

Es Caló de Sant Agustí

MAP P.100, POCKET MAP D16
Bus #2 from La Savina, mid-May to Oct daily; Nov to mid-May Mon–Sat. Bus #3 from La Savina, May–Oct daily. Bus #7 from Illetes, May–Oct daily.

Nestled around a rocky niche in the north coast, the tiny cove of **Es Caló de Sant Agustí** has served as nearby La Mola's fishing port since Roman times. Sitting snug below the cliffs of La Mola, this diminutive harbour consists of a tiny, rocky, semi-circular bay ringed by the rails of fishing huts. It's a pretty enough scene, but there's no real reason to stop other than for the excellent fish restaurant, *Restaurante Can Rafalet* (see page

141) and good value hostal of the same name (see page 119).

The shallow water surrounding Es Caló does offer decent snorkelling; head for the heavily eroded limestone rocks that ring the bay to the south. If you're after a beach, scramble 300m over the rocks (or take the signposted turn-off from the highway) to the inviting sands at **Ses Platgetes**.

La Mola

MAP P.100, POCKET MAP D16
Bus #2 from La Savina, mid-May to Oct daily; Nov to mid-May Mon–Sat. Bus #3 from La Savina, May–Oct daily.

The knuckle-shaped tableland of **La Mola**, the island's eastern tip, is the most scenic part of Formentera, combining dense forest with traditionally farmed countryside. La Mola's limestone promontory looks down on the rest of the island from a high point of 192m, and there are stunning views across the ocean from the steep cliffs that have given the area's inhabitants protection on three sides since it was first settled around 2000 BC.

From Es Caló de Sant Agustí, the highway's steep incline continues

Es Caló de Sant Agustí

past the Mar i Land turn-off, winding through Formentera's largest forest via a series of hairpin bends. At the 14km marker is the *El Mirador* restaurant (see page 110), from where there are sublime sunset views, after which the road levels out.

Mar i Land

MAP P.100, POCKET MAP D16
Bus #2 from La Savina, mid-May to Oct daily; Nov to mid-May Mon–Sat. Bus #7 from Illetes, May–Oct daily.
Close to the highway's 13km marker, you can turn off right for the upmarket enclave of **Mar i Land** (also spelled **Maryland**), signposted Platja des Copinar and Hotel Riu, where two huge hotel complexes spill down the hillside to the eastern most section of Platja de Migjorn (see page 107). This section of shoreline known as Es Arenals is usually the most crowded spot on the southern coast.

Parallel to the shore, a wooden boardwalk weaves west through the sand dunes providing a scenic route between beach bars, while to the east the soft sand soon gives way to flat rocks at the sublimely located *Bartolo chiringuito*.

Far de la Mola lighthouse

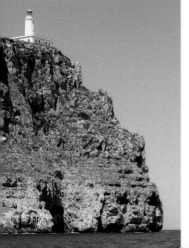

Although there are lifeguards on duty here between May and September, take great care if you go for a swim as the currents can be unpredictable.

El Pilar de la Mola

MAP P.100, POCKET MAP E16
Bus #2 from La Savina, mid-May to Oct daily; Nov to mid-May Mon–Sat. Bus #3 from La Savina, May–Oct daily.
The region's solitary village, **El Pilar de la Mola** is a modest, pleasantly unspoiled settlement strung along the main highway. Most of the time it's a subdued place, though there's a flurry of activity on Wednesdays and Sundays in the summer season, when an **art market** (May to late Sept 4–10pm) is held in the village's small central plaça. Much of the jewellery and craftwork is made locally, and tends to be far more imaginative than the offerings on sale in Ibizan hippy markets; there's usually live music towards the end of the day as well. Two hundred metres east of the market plaça is the village church, **Església del Pilar de la Mola**, built between 1772 and 1778 to a typically Ibizan minimalist design.

Far de la Mola

MAP P.100
Bus #2 from La Savina, mid-May to Oct daily; Nov to mid-May Mon–Sat. Bus #3 from La Savina, May–Oct daily.
It's a quick straight dash through flat farmland, planted with hardy vines, to the **Far de la Mola** lighthouse, set in glorious seclusion at Formentera's easternmost point, Punta de la Mola. The whitewashed structure, which has a 37-kilometre beam, is something of a local landmark, and was the inspiration for the "lighthouse at the end of the world" in Jules Verne's novel *Journey Around the Solar System*. Verne was obviously taken by the wild isolation of the site, and there's a stone monument to him beside the house. There's also an excellent café-bar here, *Codice Luna*, who put on full moon parties once a month plus DJs on market days (Wed & Sun).

Shops

Janne Ibiza

MAP P.100

C/ Punta Prima, Edificio Mar de Pujols 7,
Es Pujols. ☎ 971 328 963, ⓦ janneibiza.es.
June–Sept daily, usually 11am–1.30pm &
5pm–midnight.

Designer shop selling bright,
highly-patterned bikinis for
around €80, but prices include
a cut-to-fit service plus as many
embellishments as you wish; the
workshop at the back of the shop
is stuffed with beads, materials and
sequins in all imaginable colours.
Good end of season sales.

Majoral

MAP P.100

Av. de la Mola 89, El Pilar de la Mola.
☎ 971 327 516, ⓦ majoral.com. Mon, Tues
& Thurs–Sat 10am–2pm & 4.30–8.30pm,
Wed 10am–2pm & 4.30–9.30pm, Sun
4.30–9.30pm.

Stylish jewellery created by local
designer Enric Majoral and his
son, Roc. Designs are modern but
left unpolished giving a natural,
antique gold and silver matt effect.
The shop, built in the style of an
old finca, is an attraction in its own
right, with the metal workshop on
view to the public.

Restaurants and cafés

Beso Beach

MAP P.100

Platja de Cavall d'en Borràs, Illetes, Parc
Natural de Ses Salines. ☎ 971 324 572,
ⓦ besobeach.com. May–Oct daily for lunch
1–6pm, snacks from 7–10.30pm.

As the sign says: *no hay verano sin
beso* (there's no summer without
Beso – a kiss). Providing superb
quality Mediterranean and Basque
cuisine (marinated rock mussels
€21.50, paella with scarlet prawns
€35) and perhaps the best beach
party vibe in Formentera – DJs

Majoral

play Balearic beats and house
all day with things getting fairly
raucous from 4pm – it's always
busy and you'll need to book up to
3 weeks in advance at the height of
summer.

Blue Bar

MAP P.100

C/ San Ferran-La Mola, Platja de
Migjorn km 8. ☎ 666 758 190,
ⓦ bluebarformentera.com. May to mid-Oct
daily noon–1am.

Chilled-out beachside bar-
restaurant with an outstanding
Mediterranean/Asian fusion menu,
such as sirloin steak tataki with
baby vegetables (€24.50). Great for
ambient tunes, endless sea views
and cocktails under the stars.

Café del Lago

MAP P.100

Av. Mediterránea 20, La Savina. ☎ 971
323 187, ⓦ cafedellago.es. May–Oct daily
9am–1am.

Elegant café-restaurant very near
the port with a stylish interior and
a beautiful terrace with stunning
views of boats bobbing on the
turquoise waters of Estany des Peix.
Great for breakfast, pizza (try their

Fonda Pepe

speciality, Sa Pinxa, with bacon, scrambled egg and asparagus, €15) and a good range of mains, such as tuna tataki (€22).

El Mirador

MAP P.100
Ctra. La Mola, km 14.3, La Mola. ☎ 971 327 037. May–Oct daily 10am–11pm, midnight in high season.
Popular, moderately priced spot with jaw-dropping panoramic views over the entire western half of the island from its terrace, and an inexpensive menu – the *ensalada de bescuit* (prepared with local bread and dried fish, €10.50) is a Formenteran speciality and the paellas (from €17, min. 2 people) and grilled meats are also excellent.

El Pirata

MAP P.100
Platja de ses Illetes, Parc Natural de ses Salines. ☎ 971 324 064, ⓦ kioskoelpirata. com. April–Oct daily 9am–sunset.
At the southern end of Illetes beach, *El Pirata* has plenty of beach-facing terrace tables, a large bar plus a more formal dining area. The bar serves simple pizzas and baguettes from €10 plus the usual range of drinks and cocktails while the restaurant serves up fish and rice dishes for around €35pp. The bar gets very lively in high season and dancing on tables is not uncommon.

Fonda Pepe

MAP P.100
c/Major 68, Sant Ferran. ☎ 971 328 033. Bar May–Oct daily 9am–4am, restaurant May–Oct daily 7–noon.
Steeped in hippy folklore, this idiosyncratic drinking den still flies the flag for flower power, its walls covered with photos and doodles from the 1960s. In summer the seats outside are packed with visitors revelling in the trippy nostalgia, particularly on Friday evenings when live music is played in the square above (see page 104).

Fonda Platé

MAP P.100
C/ Sant Jaume 1, Sant Francesc. ☎ 971 322 313. Easter–end Oct, daily 10am–2am.
A welcoming, traditional café with a large interior, a charming vine-shaded patio and a buzzy, local feel. Serving up snacks, sandwiches and light meals, such as courgette lasagne with rosemary pesto (€13) or wok-fried prawns and vegetables (€14.50).

Gecko Beach Club

MAP P.100
Platja de Migjorn, Ca Marí. ☎ 971 328 024, ⓦ geckobeachclub.com. May–Oct.
Picture-postcard location on Platja Migjorn. The restaurant (daily 1–4pm & 8–11pm) serves Mediterranean cuisine (salmon tartar €21, monkfish and king prawn skewer €28) while the swanky beach club is set around a decked pool area where DJs play a mix of chillout and deep house. You'll need to reserve the Bali beds (€150, includes bottle of cava and seasonal fruit) and loungers (€35pp) well in advance in high season.

Kiosko 62

MAP P.100

Platja Ca Marí. May–Oct daily 10am–sunset, Nov–April Fri–Sun & holidays 10am–sunset.

Beach shack offering simple snacks and a wilder, more authentic Formentera *chiringuito* experience, where the drinks (including their speciality, pomada, €8) are served in plastic cups and the water laps your toes. Music is folk-indie rather than Balearic beats and there's a 10 percent discount for those who arrive by bicycle. Open all year, weather permitting.

La Vermutería

MAP P.100

Av. La Mola 36, La Mola. ☎ 971 327 089. May–Nov noon–5pm & 7pm–midnight.

Formentera's first vermouth specialist has 10 types of vermouth and over 50 Spanish wines on offer. The tapas menu is well above average, with much of the produce sourced from the organic kitchen garden at the back. Try the ginger squid (€12.50), the foie mi-cuit with vermouth (€9.50) or one of the local cheeses made in La Mola.

Macondo

MAP P.100

C/ Major 67, Sant Ferran. ☎ 971 329 069, Ⓦ macondoformentera.com. Easter–Oct, daily 1–4pm & 7.30pm–1am.

Highly recommended pizzeria serving giant pizzas from €10 in the evenings and pizza/pasta menus (pizza or pasta dish plus drink) for €12 at lunch. Gets lively at night when there's live music. It's not possible to reserve so you'll need to arrive early to bag a table.

Restaurante Can Rafalet

MAP P.100

Es Caló de Sant Agustí ☎ 971 327 077, Ⓦ canrafalet.es. June–Sept daily 1–11.30pm, May & Oct 1–4pm & 7–11pm.

Elegant and fairly formal fish restaurant with views over Es Caló bay. The menu includes *bullit de peix* (served in two courses, €32.75) and local fish like mero and dorado. There's also a casual, inexpensive bar next door whose speciality is *pa amb coses* ('bread and things'), which could be ham, tortilla, olives or cheese, for around €12 per person.

Club

Tipic

MAP P.100

Av. Miramar 164, Es Pujols. ☎ 676 885 452, Ⓦ clubtipic.com. July & Aug daily 1–6am, May, June & Sept Tue, Thu & Sat 1–6am. Entrance around €30 depending on event, more for VIP.

Stylish, well-regarded club, owned and run by Italians with excellent connections to the global house and techno scene. It's an intimate place with stylish decor, a powerful sound system and a terrace and chillout zone.

Tipic

ACCOMMODATION

Hotel Mirador Dalt Vila

Accommodation

Decent accommodation in Ibiza and Formentera can be eye-wateringly expensive, and hard to come by, in high season. However, cheaper options are available especially if you book ahead and out of season, and as a general rule you get more for your money in Santa Eulària and the northwest of Ibiza than elsewhere, with the exception of the budget hotels around Sant Antoni and Platja d'en Bossa, which tend to be cheap for the wrong reasons. Formentera is expensive all over and all season. A *hostal* is not a hostel in the budget sense but usually a smaller, independently-run hotel with private rooms. *Agroturimsos* have proliferated in recent years and are rural hotels that adhere to a set of criteria, such as the ratio of developed to undeveloped, rural land. Many visitors prefer to stay in private homes and villas and this can be a great option, particularly for larger groups.

Ibiza town and around

HOSTAL GIRAMUNDO MAP p.28, POCKET MAP B4. C/ Ramón Muntaner 55, Figueretes. ☎ 971 307 640, Ⓦ hostalgiramundoibiza.com. April–Oct. A brightly coloured, backpacker haven very close to Figueretes beach and a 10min walk from the centre. Bonuses include rooms with balconies, lockers, a DVD room, a shared kitchen and a popular in-house bar. Cheaper rooms with shared bathroom available. €140

HOSTAL JUANITA MAP p.30, POCKET MAP C3. C/ Joan d'Austria 17, Ibiza Town. ☎ 971 314 828, Ⓦ hostaljuanita.com. Mid-March to Oct. A well-located hostal with clean rooms, some en suite (€40 more) on a quiet street a 5min walk from the main drag. The highlight is the rooftop terrace with fantastic views across Dalt Vila, loungers and a cheap bar. €120

HOSTAL MAR BLAU MAP p.30 Puig des Molins ☎ 971 301 284, Ⓦ marblauibiza.com. May–Oct. Great value, family-run hotel in a superb location, a short walk from the centre of Ibiza Town and the beaches at Figueretes. Rooms are simple, clean and spacious, all en suite, most with a large terrace. There's no restaurant, entertainment or DJs, but plenty of peace and quiet and a large communal t=errace providing wonderful sea views. €100

HOSTAL PARQUE MAP p.30, POCKET MAP A7. Plaça des Parc 4, Ibiza ☎ 971 301 358, Ⓦ hostalparque.com. This fine hotel enjoys a superb location overlooking one of Ibiza Town's prettiest squares and has a popular café-restaurant serving snacks, sandwiches and mains, such as the Wagyu hamburger with smoked aubergine (€14.50). The a/c rooms are not large, but have very high

Accommodation prices

The **price range** given in accommodation reviews indicates the cost of the cheapest double room in high season (June–Sept) – note that prices may be even higher in August. Open all year unless indicated otherwise.

quality fittings, fine bed linen, shower zones and flat-screen TVs. On the roof, the three designer suites enjoy private sun terraces. €160

HOTEL ES VIVÉ MAP p.28, POCKET MAP A5. C/ Carles Roman Ferrer 8, Figueretes ☎ 971 301 902, ⓦ hotelesvive.com. **May–Oct.** Popular art deco hotel with an attractive decked pool area, three very hip bars, a roof terrace, a fine restaurant and a wellness area offering massages, treatments and a spa. But prepare yourself for small, if neat rooms, steep prices and a four-night minimum stay between Thursdays and Mondays in high season. €320

HOTEL LUX ISLA MAP p.28, POCKET MAP G1 C/ Josep Pla 1, Platja Talamanca ☎ 971 313 469, ⓦ luxisla.com. **Easter–Oct.** An excellent deal, this small, modern hotel is located just behind Talamanca Beach, about 2km from Ibiza Town. The rooms are bright, attractive and comfortable, most with balconies and sea views. You'll find a decent café-restaurant downstairs, as well as a pleasant garden and terrace area. There's no pool but you're moments from the beach. €160

HOTEL MIRADOR DALT VILA MAP p.30, POCKET MAP C8. Plaça d'Espanya 4, Dalt Vila. ☎ 971 303 045, ⓦ hotelmiradordaltvila.com. **Easter–Oct.** Family mansion house converted into a luxury, five-star hotel located within the walls of Dalt Vila. Includes a small swimming pool, a terrace bar, an excellent restaurant and one of the most important art collections in Ibiza. €520

NOBU HOTEL IBIZA BAY MAP p.28, POCKET MAP G1. Camí Ses Feixes 2, Talamanca. ☎ 971 192 222, ⓦ nobuhotelibizabay.com. **May–Oct.** For years, Ibiza had only the one 5-star hotel (*Na Xamena* in Sant Miquel) but recently that number has grown to over ten, with *Nobu* the most famous and spectacular addition to the list. Boasting 152 rooms, two swimming pools and four restaurants (including the eponymous *Nobu* and the modern Mexican-fusion *Peyotito*)

it's undoubtedly impressive, but there's something of the business hotel about it, which sits oddly in largely rough-around-the-edges Talamanca. €590

OCEAN DRIVE MAP p.28, POCKET MAP F2. Port Esportiu, Marina Botafoc. ☎ 971 318 112, ⓦ odoceandrive.com. Smart Miami-style art deco hotel in Marina Botafoc, famous for the live music events, art exhibitions and fashion shows held over the summer at its stylish Sky bar. The hotel's Friday 'Burger meets Gin' evenings are a classic among winter residents. Breakfast included. €350

RYANS LA MARINA MAP p.30, POCKET MAP C7. C/ Andenes 5, La Marina ☎ 971 310 172, ⓦ ryans.es/ryans-la-marina/. **Mid-April to Oct.** Portside hotel in the heart of the action, so noise may be an issue in high season. Rooms are light and stylish, all with a/c and TV, and many with balconies facing the harbour. Downstairs the walls of the sports bar and café are decorated with comic and film artwork, giving a bright, youthful feel to the place. *Ryans* has sister hotels in Figueretes and Dalt Vila. €180

URBAN SPACES IBIZA MAP p.30, POCKET MAP B3. Via Púnica 32, Ibiza Town. ☎ 601 199 302, ⓦ urbanspacesibiza.com. A hotel for art lovers in the centre of Ibiza Town, with colourful Andy Warhol and Roy Lichtenstein-inspired murals painted directly onto the walls. Each room has a different design, all have a terrace. There's also a pleasant garden area and small swimming pool at the back, plus a bar-café downstairs and a striking roof terrace. €175

VARA DE REY GUEST HOUSE MAP p.30, POCKET MAP A7. Passeig Vara de Rey 7, Ibiza Town ☎ 971 301 376, ⓦ hibiza. com. **Closed Jan & Feb.** Housed in an attractive former mansion, the creatively decorated rooms echo the building's grandiose charm. You'll need to climb several flights of stairs but there's a winch for your bags. Rooms all have washbasins; most bathrooms are shared. Streetside rooms can be a little noisy in high season. €140

The east

AGUAS DE IBIZA MAP p.45 C/Salvador Camacho s/n, Santa Eulària. ☎ 971 319 991, Ⓦ aguasdeibiza.com. Stylish 5-star hotel, restaurant and spa that manages to be both luxurious and relaxed. The roof-top bar and terrace (open to non-guests) offers fantastic views across the beautiful bay of Santa Eulària. **€470**

CAMPING CALA NOVA MAP p.45 Cala Nova ☎ 971 331 774, Ⓦ campingcalanova.com. May–Oct. Behind Cala Nova beach, and a short walk from Es Canar, this is an attractive campsite with good facilities and well-kept shared bathrooms. Tent plots (you'll need to bring your own tent) cost €20 for one person in high season, €29 for two. Teepees are €50 for two people. The bungalows, at €65 for two people, have their own bathroom and mini kitchen.

CAMPING VACACIONES ES CANA MAP p.45 Av. Es Caná s/n, Es Canar ☎ 971 332 117, Ⓦ campingescana.com. May–Oct. Popular with families, this site is close to Es Canar beach and has good facilities: a pool, laundry, security boxes and a bar/restaurant in July & August. Bungalows with private bathroom start from €120 for five people in high season, plus €20 cleaning fee. The cabins are €40 for two people, the teepees €57 for two people and the tent plots (bring your own tent) are €36 for two people.

CA'S CATALÀ MAP p.46 C/ del Sol s/n, Santa Eulària. ☎ 971 338 649, Ⓦ cascatala.com. May–Oct. Friendly, English-run hotel set on a quiet street in the heart of Santa Eulària, close to restaurants, shops and beaches. The thirteen (mostly en suite) rooms are comfortable and simply furnished, and there's a delightful courtyard shaded by palms, with a small pool and sun terrace. Adults only. **€135**

CAN CURREU MAP p.45 Ctra. Sant Carles km12, Sant Carles. ☎ 971 335 280, Ⓦ cancurreu.com. Immaculate rural hotel, spa and restaurant in a beautiful setting just outside Sant Carles. The sixteen rooms, each with their own private terrace, are tastefully decorated in traditional rustic style yet with modern, comfortable furnishings. With wide-reaching views across the surrounding countryside, the overall feeling is one of space and tranquillity. Breakfast included. **€325**

The northwest

ATZARÓ MAP p.58 Ctra. Sant Joan km 15. ☎ 971 338 838, Ⓦ atzaro.com. Spectacular agroturismo centred on a 400-year-old Ibiza finca. Scattered around its extensive grounds are one of Ibiza's finest spas, a 40-metre lap pool and separate main pool, an open-air restaurant and lovely gardens, planted with jasmine, palms, orange trees and lavender. Atzaró also operates as a cultural centre, hosting art exhibitions, fashion shows and festivals; see website for details. Low season rates are very good value. **€495**

CAN MARTÍ MAP p.58 2km south of Sant Joan ☎ 971 333 500, Ⓦ canmarti. com. April–Oct. Set over 18 hectares in a secluded valley, this peaceful agroturismo is Ibiza's own Garden of Eden, bursting with trees, plants and herbs of all kinds, complete with a family of donkeys and a natural swimming pool. Adhering to strict environmental principles, the finca has been renovated in a traditional Ibizan style with Arabic touches; it has its own hammam (open to non-guests) and breakfast, sourced from the garden, is served by a beautiful Moroccan gazebo. **€250**

ES CUCONS MAP p.58 Camí des Plà de Corona km 1, Santa Agnès. ☎ 971 805 501, Ⓦ escucons.com. Easter–Oct. One of Ibiza's finest country hotels, enjoying a wonderfully peaceful setting in the high inland plain of Santa Agnès. All the fourteen rooms and suites in this converted seventeenth-century farmhouse are stylish and comfortable, with beamed ceilings, views and all mod cons. There's also an excellent restaurant open to non-guests, a pool and lovely gardens. Breakfast included. **€300**

HACIENDA NA XAMENA MAP p.58 Na Xamena s/n, Sant Miquel. ☎ 971 334 500, ⓦ haciendanaxamena-ibiza.com. May–Oct. Ibiza's first five-star hotel is set in a spectacular remote location high above the rugged northwest cliffs. The rooms are spacious, most with terraces and a jacuzzi aligned for sunset-watching, and there are three swimming pools and large play area for kids. Only the Mediterranean restaurant and the sauna/spa, complete with jets and cascades, are open to non-guests. **€535**

HOTEL GARE DU NORD MAP p.58 C/ de sa Calla 11, Sant Joan. ☎ 619 251 106, ⓦ garedunordibiza.com. Easter–Oct. Small, boutique hotel with nine nicely decorated light, bright rooms, all en suite and with balcony. Downstairs is a pleasant bar and garden restaurant serving Spanish-fusion specialties such as Iberian pork with rosemary, asparagus and teriyaki sauce (€21.50). **€140**

HOSTAL LA CIGÜEÑA MAP p.58 S'Arenal Petit 36, Cala Portinatx. ☎ 971 320 614, ⓦ laciguenya.com. May–Oct. Very popular family-run hostal in a great location in Portinatx with excellent value rooms, which come equipped with a/c, kettle, small fridge and a TV. Most rooms have a sea view and the large rooms have a large terrace. There's also a swimming pool, a self-service laundry and free bikes for guests to use. Prices are on a half board basis (breakfast and dinner excl. drinks). **€120**

Sant Antoni and around

APARTHOTEL MARITIM MAP p.70 C/ Madrid 16, Port d'es Torrent. ☎ 971 340 750, ⓦ clubmaritim-ibiza.com. May–Oct. Excellent value budget hotel in a relatively peaceful part of San An but within easy reach of all amenities. The rooms are certainly not glamorous, but they're clean and spacious and the extensive grounds include two pools, a gym, a bar and a tennis court. Studio apartments with kitchenette are also available, a good option for those on a budget. Doubles **€90**, studio **€100**

CAMPING CALA BASSA MAP p.70, POCKET MAP B12. Ctra. Cala Bassa. ☎ 971 344 599, ⓦ campingcalabassa. com. Easter–Oct Beautiful grassy site with plenty of shade just 250m from Cala Bassa beach, with full facilities, including a restaurant. Mobile homes sleeping two to four (€100), Bengali wooden bungalows for four (€90) and ready erected tents for four (€90) are also available. Regular buses and boats run to and from Sant Antoni in the daytime, but you'll need your own transport or a taxi at night.

HOSTAL LA TORRE MAP p.70 Cap Negret 25, 3km north of Sant Antoni ☎ 971 342 271, ⓦ latorreibiza.com. Superbly situated above a rocky shelf and with direct sunset views, this relaxed hotel has tastefully furnished rooms facing a little garden. But the main draw is the magnificent sea-facing terrace area, perfect for drinks and meals while gawping at the setting sun. Central Sant Antoni is 3km to the south while Cala Gració is just a short walk away. DJs play from sunset to midnight every night in summer. **€262**

IBIZA ROCKS HOTEL MAP p.72, POCKET MAP F7. C/ Cervantes 27, Sant Antoni. ☎ 971 347 774, ⓦ ibizarocks.com. May–Sept. Groundbreaking hotel-event brand that shook Ibiza's dance foundations by staging rock gigs at a time when electronica was king. Ibiza Rocks gigs used to be held in bars around San An, but the brand acquired this huge 350-room hotel complex in 2008 and events – free for guests – are now staged around the large central pool area. In the last couple of years, the mood has shifted towards DJs and day-time parties (coinciding with earlier licensing laws meaning game over by 10pm) with names like Elrow, Clean Bandit and Sean Paul now reflecting the tastes of the clientele, the majority of whom are under 25. Rooms are basic, functional and en suite and all have twin beds – with a mix of event (€60 more) and non-event views available. **€180**

PURPLE HOTEL MAP p.72, POCKET MAP F7. C/ d'Antoni Riquer 23, Sant Antoni. ⓦibizafeeling.com/purple, ☏ 971 340 284. April–Oct. Describing itself as 'more than gay friendly', this lovely boutique hotel was the first in Ibiza to dedicate itself exclusively to the LGBT market, although its clean, bright rooms attract plenty of straight guests too. All rooms are en suite, with balcony or terrace, and there's a pleasant swimming pool and terrace-garden at the back. The café-bar is open to the public (daily 9am–11pm) and serves salads, burgers and stir-fries for around €8. Breakfast included. **€140**

The south

CAN XUXU MAP p.84 4km west of Sant Josep, off Av. Cala Tarida. ☏ 971 801 584, ⓦcanxuxu.com. May–Sept. Beautifully restored finca run as an exclusive, luxury hotel situated on a hectare of Sant Josep hillside amid luscious landscaped tropical gardens. The location is very private with great views and sunsets over Cornillera in the distance. The finca has been restored maintaining its original features but decorated with pieces from the owners' travels, mainly Indonesia, hence the name of some of the rooms. **€440**

HOSTAL BOUTIQUE SALINAS MAP p.84 Ctra. Sa Canal km 5, Ses Salines ☏ 971 307 640, ⓦboutiquehostalsalinas.com. May–Oct. Small, family run boutique hotel close to Salines beach. Rooms are tastefully decorated, some with a large terrace overlooking the nature reserve, and downstairs the cool bar and restaurant hosts chilled DJs and lounge music. Usually a 5-night minimum stay but worth checking. **€220**

HOSTAL CALA MOLÍ MAP p.84, POCKET MAP A13. Av. de Cala Molí, 1km south of Cala Molí ☏ 971 806 002, ⓦcalamoli. com. May–Oct. High in the hills with great sunset views, this small, welcoming hotel has attractive, good-value accommodation decorated with textile wall-hangings; all of the rooms are en suite and have their own terrace and some have a lounge (€50 more), or overlook the sea. There's a small pool,

direct access to small beach, and breakfast is included. **€135**

HOTEL GARBI MAP p.84 C/ de la Murtra 5, Platja d'en Bossa. ☏ 971 300 007, ⓦhotelgarbi-ibiza.com. April–Oct. Bang in the middle of Bossa but a world away from the ruckus outside, this spacious, immaculate hotel complex boasts two large outdoor pools, a beach bar-restaurant, a gym, spa and tennis court, an elegant lounge area and superb service. Rooms are modern, pristine and comfortable and equipped with all mod-cons and a large balcony, some with direct sea view. DJs play 'Garbi chill' throughout the day and into the night but things never get too hectic. Allegedly the most booked hotel on the island. Breakfast included. **€280**

HOTEL LOS JARDINES DE PALERM MAP p.84 C/ des Pujols d'en Cardona 34, Sant Josep. ☏ 971 800 318, ⓦjardinesdepalerm.com. May–Oct. Very tastefully decorated luxury hotel in a secluded spot at the foothill of Sa Talaia, just a few minutes' walk from Sant Josep village. The rooms have been given a minimalist makeover and exude contemporary style, each with its own private terrace. Two pools enjoy a lush garden setting, and you'll find numerous sun terraces with wonderful views across Sant Josep. The photographer Raoul Hausman, famous for documenting traditional Ibizan life, used to live at the property, then called Can Palerm, in the 1930s. **€299**

Formentera

CALA SAONA HOTEL & SPA MAP p.100 Cala Saona. ☏ 971 322 030, ⓦhotelcalasaona.com. End Apr to mid-Oct. Elegant 4-star hotel, spa and restaurant overlooking Cala Saona. Rooms are modern and comfortable and rates include access to the spa, but it's the sunset views from the spacious restaurant-terrace area, next to the large outdoor pool, that make this place really special. Breakfast included. **€325**

ES MARÈS HOTEL & SPA MAP p.100 C/ Santa María 15, Sant Francesc. ☏ 971 323

216, Ⓦ hotelesmares.com. Closed Dec. Everything from the bright, white walls to the natural, nautical materials used in the furnishings and decor make this hotel a perfect reflection of the island paradise outside. There's a spa, a small pool and garden terrace and a restaurant serving contemporary Mediterranean cuisine. **€370**

HOSTAL CAN RAFALET MAP p.100 C/ Sant Agustí 1, Es Caló. ☏ 971 327 016, Ⓦ hostal-rafalet.com. April–Oct. Overlooking a tiny fishing harbour, this hotel's spacious rooms afford magnificent sea views. With welcoming staff and a good bar and restaurant (open to the public, see page 111), it's the perfect place to unwind. **€120**

HOSTAL LA SAVINA MAP p.100 Av. Mediterránea 22–40, La Savina ☏ 971 322 279, Ⓦ hostal-lasavina.com.

May–Oct. This hip hostal is right on the beach – rooms, with their own fridges, are bright and fresh, some with balconies facing the narrow beach area that faces Estany des Peix (€20 extra). And there's a good restaurant and cocktail bar downstairs.

HOSTAL MAYANS MAP p.100 C/ Punta Prima 37, Es Pujols. ☏ 971 328 724, Ⓦ hostalmayans.es. May–Oct. Pleasant hostal in a quiet spot with bright, modern and agreeably decorated rooms, all with private bathrooms; book one on the upper floors for panoramic sea or island views. There's a pool, and the terrace restaurant downstairs, *Sa Vinya*, serves a popular buffet breakfast, as well as an Asian-influenced tapas menu in the evenings. Breakfast included. **€160**

ESSENTIALS

Sailboat in the Mediterranean

Arrival

By air

Ibiza Airport (⊚ ibizaairport.org) is
7.5km southwest of Ibiza Town. Buses
run from the airport to Ibiza Town
all year round (#10; Nov–May every
30min 7am–11.30pm, April–June &
Sept–Oct every 20min 6am–midnight,
July & Aug every 15min 6am–
midnight; €3.50), and there are also
summer services to Sant Antoni (#9;
June–Sept only, hourly 8am–1am,
July & Aug until 3am; €4) and Santa
Eulària (#24; April–Oct only, hourly
7am–midnight, €4). You can check the
latest schedules on ⊚ ibizabus.com.
Taxis charge approximately €15 to
Ibiza Town, €25 to Sant Antoni or €30
to Santa Eulària. There's no airport in
Formentera, but regular ferries and
hydrofoils shuttle between the two
islands, mostly from Ibiza Town (see
page 26).

By boat

Regular **ferries** from mainland Spain
(Barcelona, Dénia, Valencia and
Alicante) and Mallorca dock at the
Estació Marítima des Botafoc (Dique
de Botafoc) in Marina Botafoc, and at
the harbourfront dock in Sant Antoni.
From April to September, there are also
direct ferries from Dénia to La Savina,
Formentera. Boats to Formentera from
Ibiza leave from the ferry terminal on
Av. Santa Eulària in Ibiza Town, and
from the harbourfronts in Sant Antoni
and Santa Eulària, and arrive in La
Savina.

Information and maps

The best information about Ibiza and
Formentera is available from tourist
information offices on the islands,
and online. There are **tourist offices**
in Ibiza Town (see page 27), in Sant
Antoni (see page 68) and Santa
Eulària (see page 44), in addition
to the small kiosks (all May–Oct only)
located in many resorts. There are
also a couple of helpful offices in
Formentera; one in La Savina and one
in Sant Francesc (see page 99). All
staff speak English, and can provide
leaflets and accommodation lists.

Online, try the excellent Ibiza
Spotlight (⊚ ibiza-spotlight.com)
which covers everything from clubs
and party tickets to beaches and yoga,
while ⊚ ibiza.travel is the official
government website for the whole
island. For Formentera, ⊚ formentera.
es is the official government
website with comprehensive
tourist information, including Rutas
Verdes (walking routes), while
⊚ agendaformentera.cat lists up-
coming events.

All the main British **newspapers** are
widely available, as well as several
other international titles. For local
news, the DIY journalism peddled by
the *Ibiza Sun* (⊚ theibizasun.com),
a free newspaper available in all
resorts, covers the main stories in
reasonable depth (though the editorial
tone can be rabid at times). Check
out the excellent glossy magazines
published by *Pacha* and *Blue Marlin
Ibiza* (*BMI: Mag*) for features on
Ibizan life, club culture and island
personalities. *¿Qué hago hoy?* is a
useful monthly listings magazine
available for free in many of the bars,
cafés and restaurants across the
island. It's in Spanish but the essential
info is easy enough to understand. The
best **tourist map** of Ibiza is published
by Joan Costa (1:70,000) and most car
rental companies will provide you with
a reasonable free map to use.

Getting around

Ibiza has a pretty good transport network, with regular public **buses** and **boats** linking all the main resorts and towns, and there's a decent bus service on Formentera considering its tiny population. If you're planning on really exploring the islands, however, you're going to have to rent a **car**, **motorbike** or a **bicycle**, as many of the best stretches of coastline are well off the beaten track.

Buses

Buses in Ibiza and Formentera are inexpensive, punctual, and will get you around fairly quickly. Services between the main towns and resorts run roughly from 7.30am to midnight between June and late September, and 7.30am until 9.30pm in winter. Smaller villages and resorts are less well served, and buses to them are very infrequent in winter. Conversely, services to the more popular beaches and resorts are increased between June and late September. **Timetables** are available in tourist offices, printed in local newspapers and at ⓦ ibizabus.com and ⓦ busformentera. com. Note that there are far fewer buses on Sundays on all routes.

From **Ibiza Town**, there are buses to all the main towns, most villages and many resorts, and to Salines beach, all year round. **Sant Antoni** and **Santa Eulària** are the other two transport hubs, with frequent services to local beach resorts and good intra-island connections. In **Formentera**, buses shuttle between Es Pujols, Sant Ferran, Sant Francesc and La Savina, and there's also a route across the island, from La Savina to La Mola. **Fares** are very reasonable on all routes and even the longest route, Ibiza Town–Portinatx, won't cost you more than a few euros.

From the end of May to the beginning of October, the all-night **discobus** service (ⓦ discobusibiza.com) provides shuttles between Ibiza Town and Sant Antoni (#3, stops at *Amnesia* and *Privilege*); Sant Antoni and Platja d'en Bossa (#3B, for *Ushuaïa* and *Hï*); Ibiza Town and Platja d'en Bossa (#14, for *Pacha*, *Ushuaïa* and *Hï*); and Ibiza Town and Es Canar (#13-18). Buses run from around midnight until 7am (#3B runs from 4pm) and leave every 15–30min at peak times. Tickets cost €3-4. You can download the timetables onto your phone from ⓦ discobusibiza.com.

Tourist train

Kids will love the '**tourist trains**', mock steam locomotives with carriages that run several different routes around the island leaving from Santa Eulària, Es Canar, Port Sant Miquel and Portinatx. The routes take in a mixture of Ibizan culture, countryside, hills, white-washed villages and pretty beaches. Possibly the most interesting excursion is the one from Portinatx, taking in Cala de Sant Vicent and the cave of Cova Marçà at Port de Sant Miquel. Prices are €16 for adults and €8 for children. For more information, consult the advertising panels in the villages mentioned or call ☏ 607 654 321.

Boats

Plenty of **boats** buzz up and down the Ibizan coastline between May and October, providing a delightful – if expensive – alternative to bus travel. Services go from Ibiza Town to Marina Botafoc, Talamanca, Figueretes and Platja d'en Bossa; from Sant Antoni to Sant Antoni Bay, Port d'es Torrent, and Calas Gració, Salada, Bassa and Comte; and from Santa Eulària to Ibiza Town and the beaches of the northeast, including Es Canar. Fares range from

€5–20. See ⓦaquabusferryboats.com and ⓦsantaeulaliaferry.com for more info. There are ferry and hydrofoil connections between Ibiza Town and Formentera too (see page 122).

Taxis

Taxi rates on both islands are quite pricey, though all have meters and tariffs are fixed. There's a minimum charge of €4.95, with additional charges after 9pm. Taxis for hire display a green light – you can hail them on the street, wait at one of the designated ranks, or call (see numbers below). Avoid the cowboy taxi-drivers who hustle for business in high season; some have been known to work with thieves who rob your accommodation when they know you're out. From the airport, there are often huge queues at busy arrival times, though the line does go down pretty quickly.

Car and motorbike rental

Driving along Ibiza's and Formentera's main roads is pretty straightforward, though to really see the islands you'll have to tackle some challenging dirt tracks from time to time.
Daily **car-rental** costs are reasonable: for the cheapest small hatchback, expect to pay around €35 a day in July and August, which can drop to less than half this the rest of the year. Local car hire companies are cheaper than the bigger international brands but involve being shuttled to premises

outside the airport, which can be frustrating. ⓦdoyouspain.com is a useful aggregator of the cheaper local car hire companies. You have to be over 21 to rent a car in Spain.

Motorbikes and **scooters** are also a popular means of getting around the islands independently, with rates starting at around €30 for the cheapest motorbike, or from €20 a day for a scooter model. In low-lying Formentera, even the least powerful model will be adequate to get two people around, but to explore hilly Ibiza you should rent a machine above 100cc. Legally, you must be over 18 to rent a motorbike over 75cc, and crash helmets are compulsory.

Guardia Civil patrols frequently use breathalizers to test drivers' alcohol consumption. It's not uncommon for patrols to stop every other vehicle leaving the big clubs' car parks in summer. The legal limit in Spain is 0.5 milligrams of alcohol per millilitre of blood, stricter than the UK's maximum of 0.8 milligrams.

International car-rental companies

All the offices below are located at Ibiza Airport.
Avis ☏ 902 180 584, ⓦavis.es
Enterprise ☏ 902 100 101, ⓦenterprise.es
Europcar ☏ 902 105 055, ⓦeuropcar.es
Hertz ☏ 902 402 405, ⓦhertz.es

Taxi companies

Ibiza Town ☏ 971 398 483
Formentera ☏ 971 322 342
Sant Antoni ☏ 971 343 764
Santa Eulària ☏ 971 333 333
Sant Francesc Formentera ☏ 971 322 016
Sant Joan ☏ 971 333 333
Sant Josep ☏ 971 800 080
Es Pujols Formentera ☏ 971 328 016

Cycling

With few hills, **Formentera** is perfect bicycle territory and **cycling** is an easy and popular way to get around the island. Pick up a Green Routes leaflet from the tourist office or download a pdf from ⓦ formentera.es for details of some good, well-signposted cycle excursions along the island's quieter lanes. **Ibiza** is much hillier, and its roads more congested, though there are some spectacular dirt-track routes across the island, perfect for mountain biking. On both islands, renting bikes starts at around €15 a day, while state-of-the-art mountain bikes cost from €17 and electric bikes around €35.

Kandani (see below), Ecoibiza (ⓣ 971 302 347, ⓦ ecoibiza.com) and Bike Ibiza (ⓣ 627 140 824, ⓦ bikeibiza. co.uk) organize **mountain-bike tours**. ⓦ ibizabtt.com has details of serious mountain-biking events.

Bike rental

Kandani C/ Cesar Puget Riquer 27, Santa Eulària ⓣ 971 339 264, ⓦ kandani.es
Ibiza Sport C/ Soledad 32, Sant Antoni ⓣ 971 348 949, ⓦ ibizasport.com
La Cicloteca C/ Madrid 37, Ibiza Town ⓣ 971 967 009, ⓦ lacicloteca.com
Bicicletas/Moto Rent Mitjorn Various offices, Formentera ⓦ motorentmigjorn.com
Formentera Natural Various offices, Formentera ⓦ formenteranatural.com

Sports and leisure

You'll find plenty of opportunity for **sports and leisure activities** in Ibiza and Formentera, from yoga to horse riding. With a sparkling coastline never more than a short drive away, watersports are especially popular. Coastal Ibiza and Formentera also offer superb scenery for hikers. There's a large branch of the sports shop Decathlon just outside Ibiza Town, which sells every conceivable kind of sports equipment and clothing at reasonable prices, from bikinis and snorkels to hiking shoes and SUP boards (Finca Sa Olivera 3, Puig d'en Valls, ⓦ decathlon.es).

Swimming and beach life

Swimming in Ibiza and Formentera is absolutely wonderful, with several Blue Flag beaches and unpolluted, clear and – for much of the year – warm water to enjoy. Sea temperatures are at their lowest in February (around 15˚C), and highest in early September (around 28˚C).

All resort beaches, and most family-oriented bays have umbrellas and sunbeds (around €10 each per day) for rent. You'll also find pedalos, and many beaches, including Cala Bassa (see page 76) and Platja d'en Bossa (see page 91), offer banana-boat rides and other watersports (see below). The best beaches for water-based activities include Cala Vedella, Platja d'en Bossa, Es Canar, S'Argamassa, Cala Martina, Ses Salines, Portinatx and Sant Antoni.

Diving and snorkelling

The Pitiusan islands boast some of the cleanest seas in the Mediterranean. Thanks to the large meadows of endemic Posidonia seagrass, the water is exceptionally clear for most of the year and visibility of up to 30m is quite common.

Scuba diving is generally excellent, with warm seas and (mostly) gentle currents. Most scuba-diving schools open between May and September only and tend to charge similar prices. Small coves and rocky shorelines offer the most productive **snorkelling** territory: try Cala Mastella, Cala Molí and Cala Codolar in Ibiza, or Caló de Sant Agustí in Formentera. Perhaps the best area for experienced snorkellers and freedivers is the rugged northwest Ibizan coastline, at bays such as Es Portitxol and Cala d'Albarca, where there are very steep drop-offs and deep, clear water.

Scuba-diving centres

Blue Adventure c/Almadrava 67, La Savina, Formentera ☎ 971 321 168, ⓦ blue-adventure.com. Scuba school with inexpensive rates, though not PADI affiliated.

Aqua Diving Centre Ibiza Passeig del Port 18B, La Marina, Santa Eulària ☎ 693 045 723, ⓦ aquadivingcenter. com. Offering courses and trips for scuba and free diving around Santa Eulària and the east coast.

Sea Horse Scuba Diving Centre Edificio Yais 5, C/ Vizcaya 8, Port d'es Torrent ☎ 629 349 499, ⓦ seahorsedivingibiza.com. BSAC-accredited school offering dives inside the Cala d'Hort Marine Nature Reserve.

Subfari Es Portitxol beach, Cala Portinatx ☎ 971 337 558, ⓦ subfari.net. Scuba school that runs dives at many of Ibiza's remote north-coast sites.

Scuba Ibiza Marina Botafoc 101–2, Ibiza Town ☎ 971 192 884; ⓦ scubaibiza.com. Five-star PADI dive centre that offers Nitrox diving and trips into the Ses Salines Natural Park; open all year.

Windsurfing, sailing, kayaking and SUP

Windsurfing and **sailing** are popular in the Pitiuses – July and August are often the calmest months, so less challenging for the experienced, but conditions are excellent for much of the year. In early and late summer, the southern sirocco wind reaches Force 4 about once a week, while the westerly mistral can blow in at Force 6. The most popular beaches for windsurfing include Cala Martina (ideal for beginners) just north of Santa Eulària, Platja d'en Bossa and Cala Comte (for the more advanced). Exploring Ibiza's corrugated coastline by **kayak** or **SUP board** is an excellent way to get to hidden beaches and remote rocky bays; training courses and excursions can be organized locally.

Windsurfing, sailing, kayak and SUP centres

Wet4Fun Center C/ Es Cana 7, Santa Eulària ☎ 609 767 126 and Platja Es Pujols, Formentera ☎ 609 766 084. ⓦ wet4fun.com. Offering courses for sailing and windsurfing, tours for kayaks and SUP and equipment rental for all.

Fun Kayaks Ibiza ☎ 691 655 614, ⓦ funkayaksibiza.com. Great kayak tours of the north and west of the island, starting from various places including Cala Codolar, Port d'es Torrent and Cala Xarraca.

Kayak Ibiza ☎ 629 523 471. Offering kayak and SUP tours and rentals, as well as hiking and cycling. Operate from two main bases in the sumemr at Es Figueral and Figueretes.

SUP Paradise Club Náutico de Sant Antoni ☎ 666 255 803, ⓦ supparadiseibiza.com. Combined SUP and snorkelling trips to secluded coves and beaches including a special 2hr sunset trip.

Centro Náutico Formentera C/ Almadrava 60, La Savina ☎ 627 478 452, ⓦ centronauticoformentera.com. Hires out windsurfing equipment as well as sailing boats, kayaks and SUP boards.

Other watersports

Adrenaline junkies will find lots of other high-octane ways to mess around on the water, particularly in Ibiza, where you can parasail, fly-board, hire jet-skis and seabobs or take an exhilarating ride on a 360°

jetboat. Take Off Ibiza (☎ 631 738 720, ⊛ ribibiza.com), based in Sant Antoni, offers the most comprehensive range of activities, but many other companies – most of whom are on display along the beach front in Sant Antoni and Platja d'en Bossa – offer variations on the same theme.

Ocean Mania (☎ 633 208 877, ⊛ oceanmania.es) is an inflatable obstacle course located 50m out to sea opposite Ocean Beach Club in Sant Antoni. With catapults, rope swings, high dives and trampolines, it's a lot of fun for all ages (no age restrictions, but you need to be a strong swimmer, €15 for 45min). Meanwhile, Surf Lounge (☎ 971 344 797, ⊛ surfloungeibiza.com), also in Sant Antoni, has a flowrider surf machine and offers 1hr group sessions with instructors for €35 (kids 25 percent less) at their very attractive beach club (free entry). Still seeking more thrills? As the name suggests, Ibiza Cliff Diving (☎ 607 038 837, ⊛ cliffdivingibiza. com) offers classes and tours of the best spots around the island to hurl yourself off a cliff, from €70.

Boat trips and charters

Pleasure-boat trips around the coastline are highly popular, and available in most Ibizan resorts and in the towns of Santa Eulària and Sant Antoni. The Ibiza to Formentera day-trip is the most popular, stopping at Espalmador island before continuing to Platja Illetes, and often La Savina. From Ibiza Town, ferries leave from the terminal on Av. Santa Eulària in Ibiza Town (see map, p.27), while from smaller resorts there are usually deals marked up at the harbour.

Other excursions leaving from Sant Antoni harbour (all bookable from the harbourfront) include a three-hour return trip to Es Vedrà, passing Atlantis and including a snorkelling stop in Cala d'Hort, and a day-trip up the northwest coastline to Portinatx, taking in many isolated coves. From Platja d'en Bossa, Rib Ibiza (☎ 631 738 720, ⊛ ribibiza.com) organizes excellent half-day trips (€55 per person) on a rib to Espalmador and Illetes in Formentera; prices include snacks and drinks.

It need not be that expensive to **charter** a boat. Numerous companies based in Ibiza Town, Santa Eulària, Sant Antoni and La Savina, as well as in resorts such as Portinatx, offer deals on all kinds of boats, from sailing yachts and catamarans to speed boats, ribs and smaller boats that don't require experience or a licence. Ibiza Spotlight's boat charter pages give a good idea of the range companies, prices and boats available: ⊛ charters.ibiza-spotlight.com.

Hiking

Ibiza and Formentera's beautiful coastal paths and inland valleys offer exceptional **hiking**. We've detailed a few of the best walks within the Guide (see pages 36, 62 and 88), all of which have opportunities for a swim along the way; trainers, shorts and a sunhat are adequate equipment.

The quality of the Ibizan tourist offices' hiking leaflets is improving but is still not very reliable, though the signpost network that accompanies the routes is helpful. Things are better organized in Formentera, where the Green Routes network has good waymarked tracks suitable for hikers and bikers (leaflets available from the tourist offices or downloadable from ⊛ formentera.es).

Horseriding

There are several horseriding centres in Ibiza, including Club Hípico Ibiza in the south (☎ 646 500 691, ⊛ ibizahorses.es) and Ibiza Horse Valley in the north (⊛ ibizahorsevalley. com, all reservations and queries via ibizahorsevalleyassociation@

Yoga centres

Pure Om Yoga C/ Cesar Puget Riquer 21, Santa Eulària ☎ 694 421 288, ⊛ pureomyoga.net. Very welcoming yoga studio in Santa Eulària offering Hatha Flow, Ashtanga and Yin yoga classes as well as shiatsu, massage and acupuncture.
Soulshine Retreats ☎ 620 235 886, ⊛ soulshineretreats.com. Wonderfully restorative week-long retreats at a stunning luxury villa near Sant Miquel that include yoga, meditation, mindfulness, life-coaching and nutrition.
Hot Yoga Ibiza C/ de Corona 1, 1A, Ibiza Town ☎ 971 194 241, ⊛ hotyogaibiza.com. Highly regarded yoga centre with one-hour-thirty-minute classes, daily except Sat, most of which are given in a heated studio to promote a deeper and more effective yoga practice.

gmail.com), which is also a sanctuary offering a rehabilitation programme for mistreated horses. Ibiza even has its very own polo club (⊛ ibizapoloclub.es), set in a beautiful valley in Sant Llorenç and open to the public on tournament days (see website for calendar). In Formentera, Formentera Natural (see page 125) offer horseriding trips around the countryside departing from Sant Ferran.

Go-karting

There are two **go-kart tracks** in Ibiza; the hilly 300m Santa Eulària circuit, Ibiza Town–Santa Eulària road, km 5.8 (daily April–Oct 10am–sunset, Nov–March Sat & Sun 10am–7.30pm; ☎ 971 317 744, ⊛ gokartssantaeulalia.com), is the better option, with speedy 400cc adult karts, junior karts, baby karts,

mini quads and electric bikes. Much flatter and less scenic, Karting San Antonio (Ctra. Sant Antoni km 14, Jul & Aug 10am–2am, June & Sept 10am–midnight, May & Oct 10am–10pm; ☎ 971 343 805, ⊛ ibizakarting.com) is just outside Sant Antoni along the highway to Ibiza Town and has similar prices.

Mind, body & soul

Ibiza is firmly established as one of the Mediterranean's key **wellness** destinations, with a choice of centres, classes and treatments offered by acclaimed practitioners and instructors. The island itself, with its benign climate and stunning scenery, makes an inspirational base, with many classes and treatments performed in the open air in rural surrounds.

Directory A–Z

Addresses

Most street names are in Catalan, though some Castilian names survive: Plaça des Parc is Plaza del Parque on some maps. Common abbreviations are C/ for Carrer or Calle (street), Ctra. for Carretera (highway), Av. for Avenguda (avenue) and Pl. for

Plaça (square). Note that in Spain, businesses located on main roads use kilometre markers to indicate their location; so the restaurant *Lamuella* adopts the address Ctra. Sant Joan km 13. This means the restaurant is located 13km from the beginning of the road between Ibiza Town and Sant

Joan (Ibiza Town usually being the starting point in Ibiza and Sant Ferran in Formentera). Similarly, s/n stands for sin número (no number) and is used where numbering buildings is not necessary or possible, such as on empty or rural roads.

Banks and exchange

Spain's currency is the euro (€). Cashpoints (ATMs) are extremely widespread and accept all the main credit and debit cards. Bureaux de change are found in all the main resorts, often staying open until midnight, but their commission rates are higher than bank cashpoints. Virtually all restaurants and stores accept credit cards, but you may need your passport or driving licence as ID.

Clubs

Clubbing in Ibiza is inordinately expensive: entrance prices average €30–40 and can cost anything up to €80. It pays to seek out advance tickets, available in the bars of San An and Ibiza Town, which typically save you €6–10 (and include a free drink), or blag a guest pass if you can. Drinks are outrageously priced – soft drinks, including bottled water cost €8–10; a spirit with a mixer around €15. Note that none of the clubs offer free tap water to drink.

Consulate

UK, Av. d'Isidor Macabich 45, Ibiza Town ☎ 933 666 200.

Drugs

First dubbed 'ecstasy island' by The Sun in 1989, drugs are an integral part of Ibiza's clubbing scene and each night hundred of deals are done in the port bars of Ibiza Town, and in San An. Nevertheless, cocaine, ecstasy, MDMA, heroin, cannabis and ketamine are all illegal in Spain, and the police frequently search outside clubs (in car parks) and elsewhere. Those caught with small amounts (deemed for personal consumption) are often (but not necessarily) released with a caution, but in theory you could be looking at a jail term.

Hospital

Can Misses, C/ de Corona 32–36 (☎ 971 397 000), located in the western suburbs of Ibiza Town. The small Hospital de Formentera (☎ 971 321 212) is at Vénda des Brolls, Sant Francesc, and can deal with most injuries and treatments.

Post

Allow a week to ten days for mail within the EU, two weeks for the rest of the world. Post offices (correu) open between 8.30am and 1.30pm and are found in all the main towns; some souvenir shops also sell stamps.

Telephones

At the time of writing, data roaming charges are no more and the price of calls and mobile data usage for Europeans travelling in the EU are the same as if they were at home. However, prices will still vary depending on the package and provider you use and things may well change for British travellers post-Brexit, so best to check before you travel if in doubt. To call Ibiza or Formentera from abroad, dial 00 followed by the country code for Spain (34). To call abroad from Ibiza or Formentera, dial 00 followed by the country code (44 for the UK; 353 for

Emergency services

For the police, fire brigade or an ambulance call ☎ **112**.

Ireland; 1 for the US and Canada; 61 for Australia; 64 for New Zealand).

Time

Ibiza and Formentera follow CET (Central European Time), which is one hour ahead of the UK and six hours ahead of US Eastern Standard Time. Spain adopts daylight saving in winter: clocks go back in the last week in October and forward in the last week of March.

Festivals and events

In Ibiza and Formentera, traditional **festivals** and celebrations form an important part of the social calendar and present the chance for family get-togethers. Every town and village holds an annual *festa* to celebrate the patron saint of the community, with religious services and cultural events in the village square. All of the *festas* listed below follow a similar pattern, with Ibizan *ball pagès* (folk dancing) and often a display from another region of Spain, plus some live music of the soft rock variety. Bonfires are lit, *torradas* (barbecues) spit and sizzle, traditional sweet snacks like *bunyols* and *orelletes* are prepared, and there's always plenty of alcohol to lubricate proceedings. Some of the bigger events, like the Sant Bartomeu celebrations in Sant Antoni on August 24 and the *Anar a Maig* in Santa Eulària, involve spectacular fireworks displays. '*Molts anys i bons*' (many years and good ones) is the customary festival toast. The Introduction to the Guide lists other non-traditional festivals and events throughout the year (see page 8).

January

Festa de Sant Antoni Jan 17 Ibiza.
Festa de Santa Agnès de Corona Jan 21 Ibiza.

February

Festa de Santa Eulària Feb 12 Ibiza.

March/April

Semana Santa Holy Week is widely observed, with thousands assembling to watch the religious processions through Dalt Vila and up to the Puig de Missa in Santa Eulària on Good Friday.
Festa de Sant Francesc March 2 Ibiza.
Festa de Sant Josep March 19 Ibiza.
Festa de Sant Vicent April 5 Ibiza.
Festa de Sant Jordi April 23 Ibiza. Traditional fiesta in Sant Jordi, Ibiza, and book-giving throughout the Pitiuses to mark the day.

May

Anar a Maig First Sun in May Large festival in Santa Eulària with processions of horse-drawn carts, classical music, a flower festival and a big fireworks finale.
Festa de Sant Ferran May 30 Formentera.

June

Nit de Sant Joan June 23. Midsummer night features huge bonfires and effigy-burning in Sant Joan and throughout the Pitiuses, with celebrations and events both the weekend before and after.

July

Día de Verge del Carmen July 15–16. The patron saint of seafarers and fishermen is honoured with parades and the blessing of boats, especially in La Savina and Ibiza Town, where the Verge del Carmen statue is removed from the Església Sant Elm by the fishermen of La Marina and placed in a boat, which then leads a flotilla around the harbour in a ceremony to ask her protection at sea for the year ahead.

Water worship

In addition to the religious festivals, water-worshipping ceremonies (*xacotes pageses*) are performed at springs (*fonts*) and wells (*pous*) throughout the Pitiusan countryside, particularly in Ibiza. These festivals are thought to be Carthaginian in origin, and involve much singing and dancing, in order to give thanks for water in islands plagued by droughts. Some better-known ceremonies include:

July 25 Pou d'en Benet, Benimussa, 4km east of Sant Antoni.
Aug 5 Font des Verger, Es Cubells.
First Sun after Aug 5 Pou Roig, near Sant Jordi.
First Sun after Aug 28 Pou des Rafals, Sant Agustí.
Second Sun in Oct Pou de Forada, 5km northeast of Sant Antoni.
First Sat after Oct 15 Font des Xiquet, near Es Cubells.

Festa de Sant Jaume July 25. Widely celebrated throughout Formentera.

August

Santa Maria de las Neus Aug 5. Celebrated with a special mass in Ibiza Town's cathedral.
Festa de Sant Ciriac Aug 8. Small ceremony in Dalt Vila to commemorate the reconquest of 1235, plus a massive watermelon fight in Es Soto below the walls.
Día de Sant Bartomeu Aug 24. Huge harbourside fireworks display, plus concerts and dancing, in Sant Antoni.
Festa de Sant Agustí Aug 28, Ibiza.

September

Festa de Jesús Sept 8 Ibiza.
Festa de Sant Mateu Sept 21 Ibiza.

October

Verge del Pilar Oct 12 La Mola, Formentera.
Festa de Santa Teresa Oct 15 Es Cubells, Ibiza.
Festa de Sa Creu Oct 24 Sant Rafel, Ibiza. Locally made ceramics are displayed and offered for sale.

November

Festa de Sant Carles Nov 4 Ibiza.
Festa de Santa Gertrudis Nov 16 Ibiza. Includes prize animal exhibits.

December

Día de Sant Francesc Dec 5 Formentera.
Christmas (*Nadal*) Candlelit services throughout the Pitiuses, plus many arts and craft markets in the villages and towns.

Chronology

c.4500 BC Neolithic pastoralists from the mainland establish settlements in Ibiza.

1850 BC Family groups raise cattle and farm the Barbària peninsula, Formentera.

650 BC Phoenicians arrive in Ibiza.

500–146 BC Punic Era. Ibiza becomes a pivotal part of the Carthaginian Empire, with an imposing capital called Ibosim (today's Ibiza Town). Formentera is left unsettled.

146 BC After the defeat of Carthage, Ibiza achieves confederate status in the Roman Empire.

70 Formentera is resettled by the Romans, its inhabitants surviving by farming and fishing, and its population reaching 3000.

74 Ibosim renamed Ebusus, as the Romans erase Punic identity.

100–450 Agricultural land is slowly abandoned and Ibiza is reduced to being a minor trading post in a fading Roman Empire.

455 Vandal invaders briefly control the islands.

533–901 Byzantine forces usurp the Vandals. Ibiza and Formentera are subject to waves of attacks by Normans and Vikings. Gradually the Moors establish influence in the Balearics.

902–1235 The Moorish Emir of Córdoba conquers the Balearics, ushering in a period of relative prosperity and the islands are renamed Yebisah and Faramantira.

1235 Catalan conquest. Self-government brought in, Catalan becomes the official language, the islands are renamed Eivissa and Formentera.

1714 Castilian replaces Catalan control, leading to less local autonomy.

1700s and 1880s Pirate attacks diminish as Ibizan corsairs challenge Moorish buccaneers.

1890s Introduction of ferry services between Ibiza and the mainland.

1930s First tourists, mainly artists and writers, visit the islands.

1936–39 Spanish Civil War. Ibiza and Formentera are bitterly divided.

1950s Bohemian travellers return to the islands, mixing with Spanish leftists and resident artists.

1953 Thomas Cook includes Ibiza as a tourist destination for the first time.

1960s Hundreds of new hotels constructed in Ibiza and Formentera to serve the burgeoning tourist industry.

1966 Ibiza airport opens to international flights. Forty-five percent of the population still work in agriculture.

1970s Beach resorts are constructed across Ibiza. Hippies and police clash over commune evictions and nudity.

1973 *Pacha* opens just outside Ibiza Town. Annual tourist numbers reach 500,000.

1980s Wham!'s 'Club Tropicana' video is filmed in Ibiza.

1989 Ibiza dubbed 'ecstasy island' by *The Sun*.

1998 British consul Michael Birkett resigns his post, describing the drunken antics of his compatriots as 'degenerate'.

1999 Tourist arrivals top 2 million. Ibiza's Dalt Vila, Salines saltpans and Puig des Molins are declared a UNESCO World Heritage Site.

2018 Proving too expensive for local government, the island of Espalmador is sold to a private family from Luxembourg for €18 million (£16 million).

Spanish

Because virtually everyone can speak it, Spanish has become Ibiza's and Formentera's lingua franca. Until the early 1960s, when there was a mass influx of Castilian Spanish speakers, Eivissenc, the local dialect of Catalan, was the main language in the islands. Eivissenc Catalan was still spoken after the Civil War, despite the efforts of Franco, who banned the language in the media and schools across Catalan-speaking areas of eastern Spain. However, although Catalan is still the dominant tongue in rural areas and small villages, **Castilian Spanish** is more common in the towns.

Only 38 percent of Ibizan residents (the proportion is slightly higher in Formentera) now speak Catalan, a situation the Balearic government is trying to reverse by pushing through a programme of Catalanization. Virtually all street signs are now in Catalan, and it's the main medium of education in schools and colleges.

English-speaking visitors to Ibiza are usually able to get by without any Spanish or Catalan, as **English** is widely understood, especially in the resorts. In Formentera, the situation is slightly different: many people can speak a little English, but as most of their visitors are German and Italian, the islanders tend to learn those languages, and you may have some communication difficulties from time to time. If you want to make an effort, it's probably best to stick to learning Spanish – and maybe try to pick up a few phrases of Catalan. You'll get a good reception if you at least try to communicate in one of these languages.

Pronunciation

The rules of **pronunciation** are straightforward and strictly observed. Unless there's an accent, words ending in **d**, **l**, **r** and **z** are **stressed** on the last syllable; all others on the second last. All **vowels** are pure and short; combinations have predictable results.

c is pronounced 'th' as in 'thanks' before **e** and **i**, hard otherwise

g works the same way – a guttural **h** sound (like the **ch** in loch) before **e** or **i**, and a hard **g** elsewhere – *gigante* becomes 'higante'

h is always silent

j the same sound as a guttural **g**: *jamón* is pronounced 'hamon'

ll sounds like an English **y**: *tortilla* is pronounced 'torteeya'

n as in English unless it has a tilde (accent) over it, when it becomes **ny**: *mañana* sounds like 'man-yana'

v sounds a little more like **b**, *vino* becoming 'beano'

z is the same as a soft c

Basics

Yes, No, OK Sí, No, Vale
Please, Thank you Por favor, Gracias
Where?, When? ¿Dónde?, ¿Cuándo?
What?, How much? ¿Qué?, ¿Cuánto?
Here Aquí
There Allí, Allá
This, That Esto, Eso
Now Ahora
Later Más tarde
Open, Closed Abierto/a, Cerrado/a
With, Without Con, Sin
Good, Bad Bueno/a, Malo/a
Big, Small Gran(de), Pequeño/a
Cheap, Expensive Barato/a, Caro/a
Hot, Cold Caliente, Frio/a
More, Less Más, Menos
Today, Tomorrow Hoy, Mañana
Yesterday Ayer
The bill La cuenta

Greetings and responses

Hello, Goodbye Hola, Adiós
Good morning Buenos días
Good afternoon/ night Buenas tardes/ noches
See you later Hasta luego
Sorry Lo siento/ Discúlpeme

SPANISH

A few Catalan phrases

When pronouncing place names, watch out especially for words with the letter **j** – it's not 'Hondal' but 'Jondal', as in English. Note also that **x** is almost always a 'sh' sound – Xarraca is pronounced 'sharrarca'. The word for a hill, *puig*, is a tricky one, pronounced 'pootch'.

Greetings and responses

Hello Hola
Goodbye Adéu
Good morning Bon dia
Good afternoon/night Bona tarda/nit
Yes Sí
No No
OK Val
Please Per favor
Thank you Gràcies
See you later Fins després
Sorry Ho sento
Excuse me Perdoni
How are you? Com va?
I (don't) understand (No) ho entec
Not at all/You're welcome De res
Do you speak Parla
English Anglés?
I (don't) speak (No) Parlo
Catalan Català
My name is... Em dic...
What's your name? Com es diu?
I am ... English Sóc... ...anglès(a)
...Scottish ...escocès(a)
...Welsh ...gallès(a)
...Irish ...irlandès(a)
...Australian ...australià/ana
...from New Zealand ...soc neozelandès
...Canadian ...canadenc(a)
...American ...americà/ana

Excuse me Con permiso/Perdón
How are you? ¿Cómo está (usted)?
I (don't) understand (No) entiendo
Not at all/You're De nada welcome
Do you speak ¿Habla (usted)
English? inglés?
I (don't) speak (No) Hablo español Spanish
My name is... Me llamo...
What's your name? ¿Cómo se llama usted?
I am English Soy inglés(a)
Scottish escocés(a)
Australian australiano/a
Canadian canadiense/a

American americano/a
Irish irlandés(a)
Welsh galés(a)

Hotels and transport

I want Quiero
I'd like Quisiera
Do you know...? ¿Sabe...?
I don't know No sé
There is (is there?) (¿)Hay(?)
Give me... Deme...
Do you have...? ¿Tiene...?
...the time ...la hora

...a room ...una habitación
...with two beds/ double bed con dos camas/ cama matrimonial
...with shower/bath ...con ducha/baño
for one person para una persona
for two people para dos personas
for one night (one week) (para una noche (una semana)
It's fine Está bien
It's too expensive Es demasiado caro
Can one...? ¿Se puede...?
camp (near) here? ¿...acampar aquí (cerca)?
It's not very far No es muy lejos
How do I get to...? ¿Por dónde se va a...?
Left Izquierda
Right Derecha
Straight on Todo recto
Where is...? ¿Dónde está...?
...the bus station ...la estación de autobuses
...the bus stop ...la parada
...the nearest bank ...el banco más cercano
...the post office ...el correo/la oficina de correos
...the toilet ...el baño/ aseo/ servicio
Where does the bus to...leave from? ¿De dónde sale el autobús para...?
I'd like a (return) ticket to... Quisiera un billete (de ida y vuelta) para...
What time does it leave? (arrive in...)? ¿A qué hora sale? (llega a...)?
What is there to eat? ¿Qué hay para comer?

Days of the week

Monday lunes
Tuesday martes
Wednesday miércoles
Thursday jueves
Friday viernes
Saturday sábado
Sunday domingo

Numbers

1 un/uno/una
2 dos
3 tres
4 cuatro
5 cinco
6 seis
7 siete
8 ocho
9 nueve
10 diez
11 once
12 doce
13 trece
14 catorce
15 quince
16 dieciséis
17 diecisiete
18 dieciocho
19 diecinueve
20 veinte
21 vientiuno
30 treinta
40 cuarenta
50 cincuenta
60 sesenta
70 setenta
80 ochenta
90 noventa
100 cien(to)
200 doscientos
500 quinientos
1000 mil
2000 dos mil

Food and drink

aceitunas olives
agua water
ahumados smoked fish
alioli garlic mayonnaise
al ajillo with olive oil and garlic
a la marinera seafood cooked with garlic, onions and white wine
a la parilla charcoal-grilled
a la plancha grilled on a hot plate
a la romana fried in batter
albóndigas meatballs
almejas clams
anchoas anchovies
arroz rice
asado roast
bacalao cod
berenjena aubergine/eggplant
bocadillo bread-roll sandwich
boquerones small, anchovy-like fish, usually served in vinegar
café (con leche) (white) coffee

calamares squid
cangrejo crab
cebolla onion
cerveza beer
champiñones mushrooms
chorizo spicy sausage
croquetas croquettes, usually with bits of ham in them
cuchara spoon
cuchillo knife
dorada gilt head
empanada slices of fish/meat pie
ensalada salad
ensaladilla Russian salad (diced vegetables in mayonnaise, often with tuna)
fresa strawberry
gambas prawns
Hierbas sweet Ibizan liqueur
hígado liver
huevos eggs
jamón serrano cured ham
jamón de york regular ham
langostinos langoustines
lechuga lettuce
manzana apple
mejillones mussels
mero grouper
mojo garlic dressing available in rojo (spicy 'red' version) and verde ('green', made with coriander)
naranja orange

ostras oysters
pan bread
patatas alioli potatoes in garlic mayonnaise
patatas bravas fried potatoes in a spicy tomato sauce
pimientos peppers
pimientos de small peppers, with **padrón** the odd hot one
piña pineapple
pisto assortment of cooked vegetables, similar to ratatouille
plátano banana
pollo chicken
pulpo octopus
queso cheese
(Sa) Caleta café coffee made with brandy and orange peel
salchicha sausage
setas oyster mushrooms
sobrasada sausage
sopa soup
té tea
tenedor fork
tomate tomato
tortilla española potato omelette
tortilla francesa plain omelette
vino (blanco)/ (white/rosé/red)
rosado/tinto) wine
zarzuela fish stew
zumo juice

Glossary

ajuntament town hall
avinguda (av.) avenue
Baal main Carthaginian deity, 'the rider of the clouds', associated with the cult of child sacrifice
baluard bastion
barrio suburb or neighbourhood
cala cove
camí road
campo countryside
can, c'an, cas or c'as house
capella chapel
carrer (c/) street
carretera highway
casament Ibizan farmhouse
castell castle

chiringuito beach café-bar, which usually serves snacks
chupito shot of liquor
churrigueresque fancifully ornate form of Baroque art, named after its leading exponents, the Spaniard José Churriguera (1650–1723) and his extended family
correu post office
cova cave
Ebusus Roman name for Ibiza Town
Ecotax Balearic environmental tax; abandoned in 2004
Eivissa Catalan name for Ibiza, and Ibiza Town

Eivissenc Catalan dialect spoken in the Pitiuses; it's known as 'Ibicenco' in Castilian Spanish.

església church

far lighthouse

finca farmhouse

font spring, fountain

Ibosim Carthaginian name for Ibiza Town

illa island

kiosko beach bar or café

mercat market

mirador lookout

museu museum

parada bus stop

parc park

passeig avenue

plaça square

Pitiuses Southern Balearics: Ibiza, Formentera, Espalmador, Espardell, Tagomago and Conillera are the main islands.

platja beach

pou well

puig hill

punta point

riu river

salines saltpans

serra mountain

torre tower

torrent seasonal stream, dried-up river bed

urbanización housing estate

Yebisah Arabic name for Ibiza

SMALL PRINT

Publishing Information
First edition 2018

Distribution
UK, Ireland and Europe
Apa Publications (UK) Ltd; sales@roughguides.com
United States and Canada
Ingram Publisher Services; ips@ingramcontent.com
Australia and New Zealand
Woodslane; info@woodslane.com.au
Southeast Asia
Apa Publications (SN) Pte; sales@roughguides.com
Worldwide
Apa Publications (UK) Ltd; sales@roughguides.com
Special Sales, Content Licensing and CoPublishing
Rough Guides can be purchased in bulk quantities at discounted prices. We can create special editions, personalised jackets and corporate imprints tailored to your needs. sales@roughguides.com.
roughguides.com
Printed in China by RR Donnelley Asia Printing Solutions Limited

A catalogue record for this book is available from the British Library
The publishers and authors have done their best to ensure the accuracy and currency of all the information in **Pocket Rough Guide Ibiza & Formentera**, however, they can accept no responsibility for any loss, injury, or inconvenience sustained by any traveller as a result of information or advice contained in the guide.

Rough Guide Credits
Editor: Rachel Mills, Aimee White
Cartography: Katie Bennett
Managing editor: Rachel Lawrence
Picture editor: Aude Vauconsant
Cover photo research: Stewart Richardson

Original design: Richard Czapnik
Senior DTP coordinator: Dan May
Head of DTP and Pre-Press: Rebeka Davies

Author: Jo worked at Rough Guides HQ in London for many years before moving to the Balearic Islands in 2014 to officially start making the most of her time on earth. These days, she works in marketing and editorial, among other things, and spends her free time either halfway up a mountain or in the sea.

Acknowledgements

Jo would like to thank Iain Stewart, much of whose original text remains, the team at Rough Guides, Carmen Sánchez and Carlos Bernús Blanch at the tourist board, Tom at Can Martí, plus all the other kind folk who helped her along the way. Finally, much love and heartfelt thanks to Marie-Hélène, Jenny, Ros, Carla and Mel, and to Xavi for the language lessons, and everything else.

Help us update

We've gone to a lot of effort to ensure that the first edition of the **Pocket Rough Guide Ibiza & Formentera** is accurate and up-to-date. However, things change – places get "discovered", opening hours are notoriously fickle, restaurants and rooms raise prices or lower standards. If you feel we've got it wrong or left something out, we'd like to know, and if you can remember the address, the price, the hours, the phone number, so much the better.

Please send your comments with the subject line "**Pocket Rough Guide Ibiza & Formentera Update**" to mail@uk.roughguides.com. We'll credit all contributions and send a copy of the next edition (or any other Rough Guide if you prefer) for the very best emails.

Photo Credits

(Key: T-top; C-centre; B-bottom; L-left; R-right)

Alamy 2BL, 8, 9, 12, 15C, 16B, 18B, 20T, 21B, 22T, 22C, 22B, 23C, 35, 39, 51, 52, 53, 55, 60, 64, 65, 74, 80, 83, 91, 94, 96, 99, 102, 109, 110, 112/113
Experimental Beach 6
Felipe Ruiz Planells/Bar Can Berri 20B
Gabriele Canfora-Lagarty Photo/Tipic 111
Getty Images 1, 2BR, 4, 13B, 14/15, 14B, 17T, 33, 43, 49, 69, 81, 95, 97
iStock 5, 13T, 14/15, 19B, 20C, 29, 34, 36, 37, 42, 50, 76, 77, 82, 87, 104, 107, 108, 120/121
Jodie Shiel/Kiss My Fairy 78
Juan Sala/Patchwork 2CR, 41

La Luna Nell' Orto 66
Michele Falzone/AWL Images 24/25
Natasha Marshall/The Skinny Kitchen 79
Oda Berby/Lamuella Ibiza 67
Pernilla Parfitt/Project Social 54
Reinhard Schmid/4Corners Images 2T
Shutterstock 16T, 17B, 18T, 19T, 21T, 21C, 23T, 23B, 26, 47, 56, 61, 63, 70, 75, 86, 88, 89, 98, 105, 106
Vino & Co Ibiza 93

Cover: Ibiza Town **Marco Simoni/Robert Harding**
Cover flap: iStock. Gecko Beach **Club**. Getty Images

Index

INDEX